30 SEP 21

CETA:
Assessment of Public Service Employment Programs

WILLIAM MIRENGOFF
LESTER RINDLER
HARRY GREENSPAN
SCOTT SEABLOM

COMMITTEE ON EVALUATION OF
EMPLOYMENT AND TRAINING PROGRAMS
Assembly of Behavioral and Social Sciences
National Research Council

NATIONAL ACADEMY OF SCIENCES
Washington, D.C. 1980

NOTICE: The project that is the subject of this report was approved by the Governing Board of the National Research Council, whose members are drawn from the Councils of the National Academy of Sciences, the National Academy of Engineering, and the Institute of Medicine. The members of the Committee responsible for the report were chosen for their special competences and with regard for appropriate balance.

This report has been reviewed by a group other than the authors according to procedures approved by a Report Review Committee consisting of members of the National Academy of Sciences, the National Academy of Engineering, and the Institute of Medicine.

The study reported in this book was supported by a grant from the Employment and Training Administration of the U.S. Department of Labor. Points of view or opinions stated in this document are those of the authors and do not necessarily represent the official positions of the U.S. Department of Labor.

Library of Congress Cataloging in Publication Data

National Research Council. Committee on Evaluation of Employment and Training Programs.
    CETA, assessment of public service employment programs.

    Bibliography: p.
    1. Public service employment—United States.
I. Mirengoff, William.   II. Title.
HD5724.N348   1979   331.1'1'0973   79-24633
ISBN 0-309-02925-2

Available from

Office of Publications
National Academy of Sciences
2101 Constitution Avenue, N.W.
Washington, D.C. 20418

Printed in the United States of America

COMMITTEE ON EVALUATION OF EMPLOYMENT AND TRAINING PROGRAMS

PUBLICATIONS OF THE COMMITTEE ON EVALUATION OF EMPLOYMENT AND TRAINING PROGRAMS

The Comprehensive Employment and Training Act: Impact on People, Places, Programs (1976)

Transition to Decentralized Manpower Programs: Eight Area Studies (1976)

The Comprehensive Employment and Training Act: Abstracts of Selected Studies (1976)

Employment and Training Programs: The Local View (1978)

CETA: Assessment and Recommendations (1978)

CETA: Manpower Programs Under Local Control (1978)

iii

SURVEY AREAS AND FIELD RESEARCH ASSOCIATES

ARIZONA

Phoenix
John Hall, Assistant Professor, Center for Public Affairs, Arizona State University
Balance of Arizona
Paul L. Burgess, Associate Professor, with Jerry L. Kingston, Associate Professor, Department of Economics, Arizona State University

CALIFORNIA

Long Beach
Daniel M. Barber, Assistant Professor, The Center for Public Policy and Administration, California State University at Long Beach

Orange County Consortium
Lynne G. Zucker, Assistant Professor, Department of Sociology, University of California at Los Angeles

San Joaquin Consortium
C. Daniel Vencill, Research Associate, Center for Applied Manpower Research

Stanislaus County
Richard R. Kropp, Research Assistant, Center for Applied Manpower Research

FLORIDA

Pasco County
Pinellas County–St. Petersburg Consortium
Emil Bie, former Deputy Director, Office of Technical Support, U.S. Employment Service

ILLINOIS

Cook County

INDIANA

Gary
Douglas Windham, Associate Professor, Department of Education, University of Chicago (Assisted by Millard Duchon)

KANSAS

Kansas City–Wyandotte County Consortium
Anthony L. Redwood, Associate Professor, School of Business, University of Kansas

Topeka–Shawnee County Consortium
Charles E. Krider, Associate Professor, School of Business, University of Kansas

MAINE

Balance of Maine
Roderick A. Forsgren, Professor and Associate Dean, Graduate School, University of Maine

MICHIGAN

Calhoun County
Lansing Tri-County Regional Manpower Consortium
E. Earl Wright, Director, W. E. Upjohn Institute for Employment Research (Assisted in the Lansing Consortium by Philip L. Scherer)

MINNESOTA

St. Paul
Ramsey County
James E. Jernberg, Associate Director for Administration, School of Public Affairs, University of Minnesota

NEW JERSEY

Middlesex County
Union County
Jack Chernick, Professor, Institute of Management and Labor Relations, Rutgers University

NEW YORK

New York City
Lois Blume, Professor, New School for Social Research

NORTH CAROLINA

Raleigh Consortium
Balance of North Carolina
  Alvin M. Cruze, Director, Center for the Study of Social Behavior, Research Triangle Institute (Assisted in the Raleigh Consortium by Stephen A. Johnston)

OHIO

Cleveland Area–Western Reserve Consortium
  Grace Franklin, Research Associate, Mershon Center, Ohio State University

Lorain County
  Jan P. Muczyk, Associate Professor, Department of Management and Labor, Cleveland State University

PENNSYLVANIA

Chester County
  Harry Greenspan, Research Associate, National Research Council

Philadelphia
  Albert L. Shostack, Coordinator, New Jersey Association of Children's Residential Facilities

TEXAS

Capital Area Consortium
Balance of Texas
  Robert W. Glover, Associate Director, Center for the Study of Human Resources, University of Texas (Assisted by Paul A. Edwards)

Contents

*These chapters present the synopsis of the study and the recommendations of the Committee on Evaluation of Employment and Training Programs.

ix

APPENDIXES

List of Tables

xi

List of Figures

xv

Preface

This study is the latest in a series on the Comprehensive Employment and Training Act of 1973 (CETA) by the Committee on Evaluation of Employment and Training Programs, which was established by the National Research Council in 1974 to assess the social, economic, and political effects of that legislation.

CETA combined a score of separate manpower programs designed to enhance the employability of disadvantaged persons that had sprung up in the 1960s, and shifted responsibility for their management from federal to local and state officials. The act was a demonstration of the new federalism and the block grant approach in federal–local relationships.

CETA was hardly launched when it was overtaken by the recession of 1974. Congress responded by adding a countercyclical public service employment program (Title VI) to CETA, which authorized the creation of jobs for the unemployed in state and local governments. With public concern centered on rising unemployment, Title VI soon eclipsed the original structural programs of CETA. To monitor the effects of this new development, the committee's inquiry was broadened to encompass the public service employment program.

The committee has issued six earlier reports on its assessment of CETA. These studies have found that employment and training programs were being managed more effectively through decentralization; funds were allocated more objectively and there was greater community participation in planning than in pre-CETA days. On the other hand, there have been problems: the proportion of disadvantaged people in public service jobs

xvii

was lower than in other components of CETA, the job-entry rate of CETA participants has been lower than for comparable pre-CETA programs, and public service job creation has been diluted as some local governments tended to substitute CETA funds for local resources in supporting public service jobs.

To focus the PSE program more specifically on those most in need and to constrain job substitution, Congress passed the Emergency Jobs Programs Extension Act of 1976 (EJPEA), which limited new PSE jobs to the low-income unemployed and required that these positions be established in short-duration projects.

This study analyzes the extent to which targeting objectives of the Emergency Jobs Programs Extension Act have been achieved and the effectiveness of limited duration projects in providing useful public services. Taking the congressional objectives as given, the committee limited the scope of its evaluation to implementation of the act by federal and local officials.

The study deals with the administration and program of EJPEA and with the consequences of doubling the size of public service employment programs in a very short period. It examines whether jobs created are positions that would not otherwise exist, but does not assess the extent of substitution. This subject was explored more exhaustively in a previous report and has also been studied by other research organizations. Nor does the study examine participants' employment experience after they leave a program; this will be examined in a subsequent study.

A preliminary report on the present study, "Expanding Public Service Employment Under CETA: Preliminary Assessment," was issued in July 1978. It showed that the Department of Labor's goal of adding over 400,000 unemployed people to CETA public service employment under the Economic Stimulus Appropriations Act of 1977 was accomplished in 9 months. However, these results were achieved at the expense of some of the program redirection that EJPEA had sought. Persons hired from among the eligible applicants were still frequently not those most in need, and the work projects, although useful, were in many instances extensions of ongoing services rather than discrete new activities, and thus were susceptible to substitution.

This study analyzes in more detail the effects of EJPEA and includes the committee recommendations (Chapter 2). While this volume was being written, CETA was reauthorized for 4 years (PL 95-524) and amended in several significant respects. The report takes cognizance of these changes and attempts to appraise what their effects will be.

As in the earlier studies, the major source of data was a survey conducted through a network of field research associates in 28 areas. The sample was drawn from the universe of 450 prime sponsors and stratified by type of sponsor (six cities, nine counties, nine consortia, and four states) and by population size and extent of unemployment. The committee consulted government and nongovernment officials and used information from U.S. Department of Labor reports and other sources. Members of the committee brought to the task their own considerable backgrounds in manpower programs.

The committee is grateful to the field research associates who, representing the disciplines of economics, public administration, education, and sociology, analyzed developments in the sample areas. The committee also wishes to thank the prime sponsors, members of planning councils, officials of community based organizations, unions, employment service agencies, and the elected officials who provided information for the field survey.

This study is part of the program of the Assembly of Behavioral and Social Sciences of the National Research Council. William Mirengoff, who originated the project, is the study director. He is assisted by Lester Rindler, Harry Greenspan, and Scott Seablom. Phyllis Groom McCreary served as editor throughout the report writing. Marian Miller, Ingrid Larsen, Diane Goldman, and Susan Kendall furnished the support services.

The authors wish to acknowledge the assistance of the staff of the national and regional Employment and Training Administration of the Department of Labor who participated in committee meetings, provided program and statistical materials, and cooperated in arranging for the field study. The authors particularly wish to thank Seymour Brandwein, Director, Office of Program Evaluation, Employment and Training Administration, who contributed to the formulation of the study objectives and provided technical advice.

I wish to express my appreciation, as well as that of the authors, to the members of the Committee on Evaluation of Employment and Training Programs, who guided the project and patiently reviewed successive drafts of the report. Their contribution was particularly valuable in identifying major policy issues and formulating recommendations.

PHILIP J. RUTLEDGE, *Chairman*
Committee on Evaluation of Employment
    and Training Programs

CETA:
Assessment of
Public Service
Employment
Programs

1 Overview[1]

Public service employment (PSE) programs, once a minor aspect of the manpower systems, are now the dominant element of manpower policy. In terms of funding, PSE is now the major component of the Comprehensive Employment and Training Act (CETA), the block grant program that transferred management of manpower programs to local government. In PSE programs, federal funds are used to hire unemployed and underemployed persons for temporary jobs in state and local governments and in private nonprofit organizations such as social service agencies. PSE programs are intended to be used in two ways: (a) to enhance the employability and job skills of those who face structural barriers in the labor market and (b) to act as a countercyclical measure for expanding employment opportunities for the cyclically unemployed. However, in periods of low unemployment, the focus of manpower programs tends to be on the structural problems of the labor force, and public service jobs programs have a minor role in manpower policy. At the trough of the business cycle, PSE becomes a significant part of the countercyclical strategy and tends to overshadow the structural aspects of employment and training programs.

The Emergency Jobs Programs Extension Act of 1976 (EJPEA) tried to wed these objectives. It limited eligibility for most new public service

---

[1]This chapter presents the synopsis of the study prepared by the Committee on Evaluation of Employment and Training Programs.

1

employment positions to the long-term, low-income unemployed, those who generally face some kinds of barriers in the labor market. It attempted to meet the countercyclical objectives by requiring that new positions be in short-duration projects, distinct from the regular activities of local governments, so as to ensure that they would constitute newly created jobs.

This legislation was tested under unusually difficult conditions. An unprecedented buildup in enrollment in the public service jobs programs was initiated in May 1977—about the time when the Youth Employment and Demonstration Projects Act was passed and new programs for veterans and for improving the quality of job training were launched. Prime sponsors (the local governments that administer the programs) were under exceptional pressure to cope with them all simultaneously.

The major concerns of the Committee on Evaluation of Employment and Training Programs in studying the implementation of EJPEA and the expansion of the program were whether the public service employment program, as modified, was indeed reaching persons most in need of labor market assistance and whether the short-term project approach provided useful public services. The committee also explored a number of related questions: What has been the effect of EJPEA on federal–local relationships? How has the expansion of PSE affected institutional roles, particularly the relationship between the network of public employment service offices and the CETA system? And, finally, how were the EJPEA objectives of employing low-income and long-term unemployed workers affected by the overriding priority given to the rapid PSE buildup?

BACKGROUND

During the 1960s, three work experience programs in the public sector sought to improve the employability of the participants. The Neighborhood Youth Corps (NYC), Operation Mainstream, and the Public Service Careers program were all structurally oriented programs in a period of economic expansion and low unemployment. The NYC sought to prepare disadvantaged youth for employment by providing some job experience (mainly in schools), orientation to the workplace, and the discipline of working under supervision. Operation Mainstream provided supplemental income and useful community improvement activities for low-income older workers, primarily in rural areas. Of particular interest was the small-scale Public Service Careers program, which opened up opportunities in public employment for minorities and other disadvantaged persons.

With the decline in economic activity in the early 1970s, public service employment programs were adopted as a countercyclical measure—to provide temporary employment for the jobless quickly and to stimulate the lagging economy. The Emergency Employment Act of 1971 (EEA), enacted when the unemployment rate was 6 percent, authorized a 2-year program (known as the Public Employment Program, or PEP), to create jobs in state and local governments throughout the country, with an added boost for areas of substantial unemployment.

When the Comprehensive Employment and Training Act was under consideration in late 1973, the unemployment rate had subsided to less than 5 percent and the authorization for PEP had expired. The proposed inclusion of a public service employment title caused more controversy than any other issue during the drafting of CETA. As finally enacted, the legislation retained a modest public service employment program (Title II), but only for areas of substantial unemployment, and its emphasis was on the creation of temporary jobs leading to unsubsidized employment.

A year later, with unemployment above 8 percent, Congress added a universal 1-year countercyclical public service employment program (Title VI) to CETA. The nation's manpower policy now addressed both the structural and cyclical problems of the labor market.

As public service employment expanded, two major problems surfaced. Participants in PSE were decidedly less disadvantaged than those enrolled in employability development programs under Title I and there were growing signs that, to meet local priorities, some local governments were substituting CETA workers for government employees who normally were supported from state and local taxes—a practice incompatible with the legislative objective of expanding employment opportunities. The administration and Congress were concerned that the program had drifted away from its primary goals. The Emergency Jobs Programs Extension Act of 1976 sought to remedy this.

• To direct the program more specifically to the disadvantaged, new hires above existing (sustainment) levels, plus half of those hired as replacements, were to be long-term, low-income unemployed or welfare recipients. Prime sponsors were to make special efforts to hire four categories of eligible persons in proportion to their numbers in the eligible population—AFDC recipients, persons receiving unemployment compensation for 15 or more weeks, those who had exhausted their unemployment insurance, and others out of work for 15 or more weeks.

• To deter substitution, most of the new hires were to be employed in short-duration projects outside regular ongoing government services. Also, prime sponsors were encouraged to contract with private nonprofit organizations as well as government agencies to operate PSE projects on the expectation that these organizations would fund new activities.

The redesign of Title VI under EJPEA assumed much greater significance as the new Carter administration made expansion of the PSE programs an important part of its economic stimulus strategy.

THE BALANCE SHEET

ACCOMPLISHMENTS

Some of the goals of EJPEA and the economic stimulus expansion have, to varying degrees, been realized.

• The CETA system responded to the demands of the PSE buildup. The goal of adding 425,000 enrollees in 9 months was achieved, albeit at a considerable price. The Department of Labor acted speedily to establish regulations and procedures. Local sponsors adjusted local CETA organizations to the more complex administrative requirements for developing projects and selecting enrollees.

• In the limited-term projects, the proportion of unemployed enrollees who were welfare recipients or had income below poverty levels rose, compared with those previously enrolled in Title VI. (However, in other PSE programs, the proportion of minorities and persons with low educational attainment—groups often considered disadvantaged—declined.)

• A majority of projects established under EJPEA were in activities that would not have been funded in the absence of CETA. Further, the greater use of private nonprofit organizations as employing agencies and emphasis on hiring the disadvantaged tended to decrease the likelihood of substitution.

• As the law required, projects did provide public services that were useful. Government projects were most commonly found in public works, parks and recreation; projects conducted by nonprofit agencies were usually social service activities.

• Project enrollees were found to perform their duties as well as regular employees in similar positions.

• As a consequence of working together to recruit eligible candidates for the PSE buildup, relationships between CETA and the employment service became more harmonious and productive in many jurisdictions.

SHORTFALLS

However, the implementation of EJPEA was not without its defects.

• The targeting objective of EJPEA was compromised by a number of factors. The procedures for finding and hiring PSE participants did not ensure that eligible persons most in need would be selected. The legislative requirement that reasonable efforts be made to hire specific groups (AFDC recipients, long-term unemployment insurance beneficiaries, unemployment insurance exhaustees, and other long-term unemployed) in accordance with their proportion in the population eligible for projects was not met. In particular, the share of AFDC recipients hired was far below their proportion in the eligible population.

A significant proportion of ineligible participants were enrolled, reflecting loose procedures for verifying eligibility of PSE participants, and it was uncertain as to who was to be liable for improper enrollment.

• The increase in the proportion of economically disadvantaged persons in Title VI projects was largely offset by reductions in the proportion of other disadvantaged in Title II programs—minorities and persons with less than a high school education.

• Contrary to the original intent of the legislation, about 40 percent of the Title VI project positions were for extensions or maintenance of regular government activities. This, plus other characteristics of the projects, such as their duration, increased their susceptibility to substitution.

• The EJPEA requirement that the planning councils review and recommend projects to be funded was not fulfilled. It proved impossible for councils to review the 85,000 proposals in the time available, except in a perfunctory fashion. Moreover, the review of projects diverted time and effort from the comprehensive planning for all local CETA programs—the main purpose of these local advisory councils.

The basic objectives of EJPEA—directing the program more to persons who have been least successful in the job market and restraining substitution—were only partially achieved. They were compromised to some extent because of the pressure from the Department of Labor for rapid expansion and the tendency of localities to adapt federal programs to local objectives. In the interest of speed and of ensuring local cooperation, the definition of projects was watered down and the criteria for eligibility was liberalized. The push for larger enrollments in a short time precluded careful attention to screening PSE candidates.

Operating within the tyranny of time and other constraints, EJPEA was

CETA Public Service Employment Legislative Changes, 1973 Through 1978

Date	Act	Title	Major Provisions
December 28, 1973	Comprehensive Employment and Training Act of 1973 PL 93-203	II	Provides funds to prime sponsors and Indian reservations to hire the unemployed and underemployed in areas of substantial unemployment (ASUs) for public service jobs. Funds are allocated based on the number of unemployed in each ASU. An ASU is an area or section of an area with unemployment rates of 6.5 percent or more for 3 consecutive months. Unemployed applicants must be jobless for 30 days.
December 31, 1974	Emergency Jobs and Unemployment Assistance Act of 1974 PL 93-567	VI	Authorizes public service jobs for the unemployed and underemployed as a countercyclical measure. Funds are allocated among all prime sponsors and Indian reservations based on the number of unemployed, unemployed in excess of a 4.5 percent rate, and the unemployed in ASUs. Special eligibility rules apply to areas of 7 percent or more unemployment rates.

Date	Program	Title	Description
October 1, 1976	Emergency Jobs Programs Extension Act of 1976 PL 94-444	VI	Funds for an expanded Title VI program to be in short-duration projects. New participants for project jobs and half of those hired for replacements to be long-term, low-income unemployed or welfare recipients.
October 27, 1978	Comprehensive Employment and Training Act Amendments of 1978 PL 95-524	IID	Establishes a public service employment program for economically disadvantaged persons. Funds allocated to all prime sponsors based on the number of unemployed, unemployed in excess of a 4.5 percent rate, unemployed in ASUs, and number of adults in low-income families.
		VI	Provides temporary public service jobs when the national rate of unemployment is in excess of 4 percent. Funds allocated to all prime sponsors based on the number of unemployed, unemployed in excess of a 4.5 percent rate, and unemployed in ASUs. Half of funds allotted to be used for short-term projects.
		IID and VI	All applicants must be long-term, low-income unemployed or welfare recipients, but the standards for duration of unemployment and income differ between Titles IID and VI. Average wage set at $7,200 (compared with $7,800 previously), maximum at $10,000. A portion of allotment reserved for training. Duration of public service jobs for each participant limited to 18 months.

7

partially successful in achieving what Congress had intended—increased enrollment of the poor in public service employment projects and developing projects in activities that otherwise would not have been supported with local funds.

SUMMARY OF MAJOR RECOMMENDATIONS

In formulating its recommendations, the Committee on Evaluation of Employment and Training Programs took as its point of departure the stipulated objectives of EJPEA—(a) to direct public service employment programs to groups that, in the opinion of Congress, were most in need and (b) to improve the countercyclical impact of PSE by constraining substitution. The committee also took into account provisions of the 1978 act that reauthorized CETA for 4 years. To some extent, as in its emphasis on targeting, training, and transition, that act anticipated several of the recommendations flowing from this study. In those cases, the committee considered whether the legislated response was appropriate and how the new provisions were to be administered.

Above all, the recommendations propose more effective targeting of the PSE program—to persons most in need within the eligible population and to areas that have the largest number in need. Second, the committee believes that the project mode has had some effect in checking substitution and recommends that projects be used more extensively than contemplated by the reauthorization act.

Title IID of the reauthorization act stresses the importance of the transition of participants into unsubsidized jobs and provides for employability development services to support this objective. The committee believes that Title VI enrollees should be treated the same way. While Title VI is a countercyclical program, the ultimate objective of enhancing employability and self-sufficiency of enrollees remains central.

Major committee recommendations are summarized below. They are discussed more fully in Chapter 2, along with study findings and the issues that called forth the recommendations.

1. *Targeting.* The list of target groups that the reauthorization act requires be given consideration is too long to be effective. Congress should sharply limit the number of groups to receive preference under Title IID, the structural component of CETA. These might include persons with low educational attainment as well as public assistance beneficiaries and disabled and Vietnam-era veterans, who are already listed in the act. The Department of Labor should offer incentives to encourage selection of participants from these preference groups, and sponsors should use a

rating system to select those most in need and to give special weight to target groups.

2. *Allocations.* To achieve better distribution of Title VI funds to geographic areas that have the largest number in need, consideration should be given to including a factor in the Title VI formula that would measure a combination of income and duration of employment. Prime sponsor jurisdictions with unemployment rates of less than 4 percent should not receive any funds, except for pockets of substantial unemployment within their boundaries.

3. *Title VI Projects.* A number of committee recommendations deal with better use of projects to control substitution, enhancing the usefulness of PSE activities and the process of developing projects.

• (a) More than 50 percent of Title VI funds should be authorized for project activities and limits should be placed on the renewal of projects in order to control substitution more effectively; (b) a substantial portion of Title VI funds should be used for nonprofit organizations; (c) the definition of projects should be tightened to emphasize new activities and; (d) auditing to detect maintenance of effort violations should be intensified.

• To serve participants more effectively, Title VI projects should combine training with public service jobs that furnish marketable skills and experience. Greater stress should be placed on transition of public service employment enrollees to unsubsidized jobs.

• To ease the administrative burden of developing and reviewing large numbers of Title VI project proposals, those projects that would enroll fewer than three participants should not be treated as projects but as individual applications under regular PSE programs. The permissible administrative costs for Title IID and Title VI should be increased to allow for stepped-up eligibility verification and monitoring.

4. *Wage Limits.* To improve the method of adjusting the limit on the public service employment wage level for each prime sponsor area, the Department of Labor should refine its techniques to establish wage standards suitable for high as well as low wage areas.

5. *Federal Administration.* Appropriations and allocations of funds should be made far enough in advance to allow sufficient lead time and more orderly administration. Monitoring of eligibility and maintenance of effort by the DOL should be expanded and intensified.

6. *Local Administration.* To ensure that those most in need are chosen and that special groups are served equitably, prime sponsors should exercise more control over the selection of participants. Prime sponsors should maintain an active file of eligible applicants for public service employment and other CETA programs.

7. *Linkages.* The DOL should promote closer integration of public

service employment with employability development programs in order to serve participants more effectively. Cooperative arrangements between CETA and other human resource and economic development agencies should be developed to make better use of joint resources.

UNRESOLVED ISSUES

During the 7 years since the passage of the Emergency Employment Act of 1971, the nation has become increasingly committed to public service jobs programs as an instrument of economic and social policy. However, several unresolved issues cloud these programs and new ones arise as the scale of public service jobs programs is expanded. Among those that require attention are: (a) the appropriate limits of public service jobs programs for public policy purposes, (b) the divergent interests of national and local governments, (c) multiple program objectives, (d) the utility of PSE as a means of employability development, and (e) the incentive structure of PSE.

LIMITS OF PSE

The growth of public service jobs programs under CETA testifies to their growing importance as an instrument of national policy. The $5.7 billion spent for CETA PSE in fiscal 1978 represented 40 percent of the outlay by all federal agencies for employment and training programs. In 1978, 1 of every 20 persons in state and local governments was supported with CETA funds; in some instances the ratio was as high as 1 to 6. As PSE programs become institutionalized, they may be accompanied by a shift of part of the burden for supporting public services from the local to the federal level. PSE is also proposed as a central element in policies for combating recessions, for economic development, achieving full employment, training of the structurally unemployed, and, recently, welfare reform.

The issue is whether CETA PSE should become a program for all seasons. Can state and local government employment, which account for only one-eighth of total employment, be expected to carry the full burden of providing temporary and useful employment for the unemployed and economically disadvantaged? The question is particularly pertinent now, when the growth of state and local government employment is slowing, and when the fiscal pressures still plaguing many jurisdictions make it difficult for them to meet even essential payrolls, and there may be further cutbacks due to taxpayer revolts.

A related question is the appropriate roles of the public and private sectors in expanding employment for the disadvantaged. On-the-job training opportunities in the private sector are being stressed under the CETA reauthorization act, but the potential of private sector initiatives will not be known until more experience is gained.

PSE AND EMPLOYABILITY DEVELOPMENT

The concept behind Title IID, namely that combinations of training and public service employment may provide the kinds of skills and experience that will lead to placement in unsubsidized employment, appears to be sound. The issue is whether the kinds of activities customarily found in CETA public service jobs programs, heavily concentrated in public works and parks development and maintenance, will indeed provide the skills and experience that are transferable to the private sector where most of the participants will ultimately seek employment. Experience to date under CETA does not provide a basis for predicting success, since there has been very little training of PSE participants.

WAGES AND INCENTIVES

The CETA reauthorization act lowered the permissible average wage for prime sponsor areas and restricted wage supplementation by local governments. The intent was to encourage participants to seek unsubsidized employment by making CETA positions less attractive than alternatives. However, the change has additional implications. Besides limiting the types and quality of work projects, the change could affect the incentives for welfare, unemployment insurance, or other transfer payment recipients to participate in PSE programs. This would adversely affect the results of the targeting objectives of the act.

NATIONAL VERSUS LOCAL INTERESTS

The underlying premise of a decentralized system for administering the PSE program is that the national objective of reducing unemployment by creating jobs for the disadvantaged in the public sector is congruent with local government objectives and priorities. While this may in part be true, there are significant divergences. CETA is in fact a blend of national and local aspirations implemented by an array of federal, state, and local institutions.

- Congress establishes national policy and objectives.
- The DOL interprets the legislation, prescribes procedures for its implementation, and oversees its operation.

- State and local units of government execute the program.

Each partner in this triad, however, is motivated by its own particular interests and attempts to shape the program to these interests. To the degree that objectives diverge, the original thrust of the program may be diluted as implementation filters through departmental interpretation and local adaptation. For example, congressional emphasis is upon serving those most in need; but local governments, understandably, generally seek to enroll the most qualified persons available. For its part, the early concern of the DOL was with speedy implementation of CETA.

Local deviation from national objectives invites restrictive legislation and compliance activities which place additional strains upon the program and divert energies and resources from accomplishment of substantive goals. This issue is likely to continue since the concept of decentralization implies an element of diversity.

MULTIPLE GOALS

The issue of multiple objectives is related to the problem of diverging interests. The interests of numerous national policy shapers and local program operators are reflected in the profusion of CETA PSE goals. However, multiple goals may be inevitable in a program involving several institutions and the wide span of CETA objectives can be a source of broad constituency support.

PSE does abound with objectives, many of them competitive or conflicting, and the pursuit of one may preclude the attainment of another. Central among the PSE purposes are job creation (control of substitution) for the disadvantaged (targeting) and subsequent employment of program participants in unsubsidized jobs (transition). To maximize job creation and constrain substitution, EJPEA mandated the use of special projects outside the regular pattern of state and local government employment. But precisely because they are not in the mainstream of government employment, transition from these jobs to regular public sector jobs may be more difficult.

EJPEA also aimed at increasing the share of disadvantaged persons participating in PSE programs. This too may have adversely affected transition, since employing agencies tend to follow their usual selection practice of hiring the most highly qualified applicants available.

This is not to suggest that the problems are insurmountable. But it does call for greater clarity in the legislation and a high degree of refinement in program operations. Both may further erode local flexibility.

In effect, CETA PSE established a host of deities to whom the local sponsors must pay homage. However, offerings to one may offend others. And since all cannot be placated simultaneously, the sponsor is always in difficulty. A hierarchy that clearly identifies the primary deities would be most useful.

In fact CETA itself has developed internal inconsistencies. The most notable is the vagueness in delineating federal and local responsibility. EJPEA and the CETA reauthorization have beclouded this issue by restoring more and more control to federal officials.

2 Findings and Recommendations

This chapter presents the recommendations of the Committee on Evaluation of Employment and Training Programs. In developing its recommendations, the committee was guided by several broad considerations: the underlying objective of manpower development policy—to assist those faced with structural barriers in the labor market; the original objectives of CETA—maintaining an orderly and flexible delivery system with local accountability; and the countercyclical objectives of public service employment programs—to provide temporary jobs for the unemployed leading toward unsubsidized employment. The major considerations were the objectives of EJPEA—redirecting CETA public service employment to the goal of assisting those who have the most difficulty in the labor market and restricting substitution.

The committee's study dealt mainly with substantive aspects of the public service employment programs, but also with the institutional aspects—changes in administration and processes stemming from amendments to the act. Its findings include the effect of EJPEA on the kinds of persons selected for PSE programs and the kinds of projects developed and implemented. Most of the data were gathered during the buildup of public service employment in late 1977 and early 1978 before sponsors had faced the task of finding unsubsidized employment for the newly enrolled participants.

EJPEA was, in a limited way, a forerunner of some of the features incorporated in the CETA reauthorization act of 1978, which changed the structure and requirements of PSE. The reauthorization act extended CETA for 4 years and established two separate public service employment programs: Title IID, a permanent program combined with training for the structurally unemployed, and Title VI for cyclical unemployment. A second major feature limits eligibility in all titles to the low-income, long-term unemployed. The statute requires that half of countercyclical public jobs be in short-duration projects, a carryover from EJPEA. These provisions, along with a number of other modifications—such as defining projects to permit expansion of existing services, lowering the average wage that could be paid to PSE participants, extending project duration from 12 to 18 months, and limiting the tenure of individuals in public service jobs—reflect judgments on the part of Congress and the administration on experience with EJPEA. In developing its recommendations, the committee was mindful of the actions taken under the reauthorization act.

The findings and recommendations, which are grouped in three categories, are discussed in relation both to the conclusions of the study and to changes incorporated in the CETA reauthorization. These categories are participants, projects, and administrative and institutional roles.

PROGRAM PARTICIPANTS

Tightening eligibility criteria under the Emergency Jobs Programs Extension Act had the predictable effect of shrinking the size of the population potentially eligible for most new PSE positions—from 20.2 million persons previously eligible to 4.4 million eligible for PSE projects under EJPEA, as shown in Table 1.[1] Project participants had to be members of welfare families or low-income persons unemployed for 15 weeks or more. While prime sponsors had to choose enrollees for projects from a more disadvantaged pool of applicants—poorer, less educated, and more likely to be nonwhite than those eligible before EJPEA—there were still more than 10 persons eligible for every position available. Selection was left to local officials.

REACHING THOSE MOST IN NEED

The net result of (a) a smaller and more disadvantaged eligible population; (b) provisions requiring selection in proportion to numbers in the eligible population of AFDC recipients, unemployment insurance beneficiaries,

[1]Under EJPEA, new enrollees for Title VI public service project positions and for half of the vacancies in the regular Title VI positions were to be drawn from the low-income, long-term unemployed, estimated to number 4.4 million. Enrollees for the other half of the Title VI vacancies and for Title II were drawn from an unemployed and underemployed population, estimated at 20.2 million.

TABLE 1 Persons Eligible for CETA Public Service Employment Programs and Participants, Before and After the Emergency Jobs Programs Extension Act

	Eligibility Requirements	Potentially Eligible Population (millions)	Participants	
			Date	Number
Before EJPEA				
Title II	Unemployed 30 days or more; or underemployed	20.2	June 1976	74,000
Title VI	Same as Title II, above	20.2	June 1976	171,000
After EJPEA (October 1976)				
Title II	Same as Title II, above	20.2	March 1978	129,000
Title VI: Projects	Unemployed 15 weeks or more and member of low-income family; AFDC recipients	4.4	March 1978	347,000
Title VI: Sustainment				
Half of new enrollees for regular Title VI positions	Same as Title VI Projects	4.4	March 1978	82,000
Half of new enrollees for regular Title VI positions and participants carried over from before October 1976	Same as Title II, above	20.2	March 1978	184,000

unemployment insurance exhaustees, and other low-income persons jobless for 15 weeks or longer; (c) Department of Labor requirements for determining and verifying eligibility; and (d) selection practices of prime sponsors and employing agencies was a mixture of changes in characteristics of PSE enrollees.

• Those hired for projects reflected the more stringent requirements—a larger proportion were poor, welfare recipients, and unemployed than those previously enrolled in PSE programs. However, the proportion of disadvantaged persons hired for project positions was significantly smaller than their proportion in the eligible population. While 93 percent of the eligible population had incomes below the poverty level, only 73 percent of those enrolled in PSE projects were in this category. Similarly, the proportions of persons with less than a high school education, welfare recipients, and women were lower than their proportions in the eligible population. The least disadvantaged came off best in the recruitment and hiring process.

• The impact of the new eligibility requirements on regular Title VI "sustainment" positions was more limited because they applied to only half of new hires. There were some gains in the proportions of enrollees who were economically disadvantaged or were welfare recipients, but other changes were relatively small.

• EJPEA eligibility requirements applied only to Title VI, and not to Title II (PSE for areas of substantial unemployment). However, both programs were handled by the same sponsors and there are indications that EJPEA had an indirect effect on the selection of Title II enrollees. Labor Department data show a decline in the proportion of minorities and persons with low educational attainment in Title II programs, suggesting that sponsors might have selected less disadvantaged persons for Title II positions and more disadvantaged applicants for Title VI.

• EJPEA required that prime sponsors hire AFDC recipients, unemployment insurance beneficiaries, unemployment insurance exhaustees, and the long-term unemployed in proportion to their numbers in the eligible population. Prime sponsors, in cooperation with employment service offices, established pools of eligibles from these four groups, but most had no mechanism to ensure proportionate selection and some were unaware of this requirement. Equitable allocation of openings among various groups has not occurred. Problems in obtaining necessary data, the difficulty of matching applicants with openings, and the complexity of too many competing target groups are responsible, according to local officials. The proportion of AFDC recipients and UI beneficiaries hired was far below their proportion either in the applicant pools or in the eligible population.

• Recruitment for projects was influenced by prime sponsor policies in developing and approving projects. In half of the areas studied, sponsors advised project operators to design projects compatible with the skills of the long-term unemployed. In the remaining areas, the development of projects, and hence recruitment, tended to be demand-oriented—the activities to be performed were identified first, and the selection of qualified applicants followed.

The effect of EJPEA eligibility requirements was thus confined to certain segments of the PSE program and was diluted by offsetting changes in other PSE programs. The policies of the Department of Labor on verification of eligibility and the selection and hiring practices of prime sponsors had as much to do with changes in the characteristics of enrollees as the eligibility requirements did. Once projects were approved, employing agencies tended to choose the best qualified applicants from among those eligible, rather than those most in need.

The targeting objectives of EJPEA were frustrated by several other developments. Chief among these was the unrelenting pressure on prime sponsors to meet hiring schedules. Not only was there no time to ensure that less qualified persons would have equal access to positions, there was not enough time to adequately verify eligibility.

Short-term, low-paying project jobs had limited appeal for persons on welfare or for unemployment insurance recipients. The low participation rate of the persons who needed labor market assistance most was also attributed to the sex stereotyping of positions and reluctance to refer or hire female applicants, merit system standards that tend to favor persons with more education, and the widespread practice of preselecting qualified candidates.

Recommendations

Higher enrollment of persons most in need can be achieved by changing the eligibility requirements in the act or by tightening selection processes, or both. The CETA reauthorization act took the former approach. It established a special title (IID) to provide PSE jobs for the hard-core unemployed, using the tighter eligibility criteria introduced by EJPEA for project positions. Title VI, reserved for countercyclical public service employment, was also limited to the low-income, long-term unemployed and welfare recipients, but the criteria were loosened. Establishing a structural PSE program and restricting eligibility for countercyclical programs will help, but experience under EJPEA suggests that it is also necessary to tighten the selection processes.

The major targeting impediment is the tendency to hire the most qualified from among the eligible population. In order to direct the PSE program more closely to those most in need and to ensure equitable consideration of priority groups, the committee recommends that (1) Congress specify a smaller number of target groups, (2) the DOL offer incentives to encourage the selection of Title IID participants from these groups, (3) the DOL encourage sponsors to select participants objectively by using a rating system, and (4) the DOL require prime sponsors to establish job search orientation and training for PSE applicants to encourage and assist those who are able to do so to find unsubsidized employment. These recommendations are discussed in the following sections.

Priority Groups The four low-income groups specified in EJPEA for equitable treatment (AFDC and UI beneficiaries, UI exhaustees, and long-term unemployed) were overlaid on existing provisions of the act. The Department of Labor also set a goal for hiring veterans (35 percent of new hires), which took precedence over other requirements. But the legislation did not mandate equitable allocation of jobs among the four groups identified in EJPEA, and the hasty enrollment buildup precluded a careful balancing of the interests of each of these with the many other client categories listed in the legislation and with the priorities established by local prime sponsors.

The CETA reauthorization act of 1978 changed the targeting rules. The act states that public service jobs are intended for those who need labor market assistance and that consideration must be given to Vietnam-era veterans and public welfare recipients. But it added, by reference to Title III, a host of additional groups—offenders, persons of limited English language proficiency, handicapped persons, women, single parents, displaced homemakers, youth, older workers, and persons with limited education. And sponsors must still give equitable treatment to locally identified significant segments of the eligible population.

Too many priorities means no priorities. Identifying so many groups for special emphasis weakens the targeting thrust of the legislation and burdens prime sponsors with competing priorities. It is an unworkable requirement, particularly in the light of multiple eligibility requirements for other titles of CETA . It is too broad to have any practical effect in limiting enrollment to the most disadvantaged (see chart p. 20–21).

To ensure that those most in need are moved to the head of the queue and to be more effective in targeting to selected preference groups, *the committee recommends that the act be amended to give priority to a smaller number of categories in Title IID.* Since that title is intended for the

CETA — Changes in Eligibility and Targeting for Public Service Employment, 1973-1978

Date	Act	Title	Eligibility	Targeting
Dec. 28, 1973	Comprehensive Employment and Training Act of 1973 PL 93-203	II Areas of Substantial Unemployment	1. Unemployed 30 days or more or underemployed.	1. Consideration for most severely disadvantaged in terms of length of unemployment and prospects of obtaining a job; Vietnam veterans; and former manpower trainees. Equitable treatment for significant segments of the unemployed population.
Dec. 31, 1974	Emergency Jobs and Unemployment Assistance Act of 1974 PL 93-567	VI Countercyclical public service employment	2. Unemployed 30 days or more or underemployed. For areas of excessively high unemployment (7 percent or more), unemployed 15 instead of 30 days.	2. The same as in 1, above. Also preferred consideration for: the unemployed who have exhausted UI benefits; unemployed not eligible for UI (except new entrants); persons unemployed 15 or more weeks; recently separated veterans (within last 4 years).
Oct. 1, 1976	Emergency Jobs Programs Extension Act of 1976 PL 94-444	VI Countercyclical public service employment	3. *For half of vacancies in regular positions above June 1976 level:* the same as in 2, above. 4. *For the remaining half of regular vacancies and for new project positions:* (a) either member of low-income family, and (b) either received unemployment insurance for 15 or more weeks, was not eligible for UI but was unemployed for	3. *For half of vacancies in regular positions above June 1976 levels:* the same as in 2, above. 4. *For the remaining half of regular vacancies and for new project positions:* the same as in 2, above. In addition, equitable allocation of jobs among: members of low-income families who received unemployment insurance for 15 or more weeks, were not eligible for UI but were unemployed 15 or more weeks, exhausted UI entitlement, or were AFDC recipients. (Low-income

20

| Oct. 27, 1978 | Comprehensive Employment and Training Act Amendments of 1978 PL 95-524 | IID Public service employment for the economically disadvantaged | 5. Unemployed 15 weeks and member of low-income family; or member of family receiving AFDC or SSI. (Low-income defined as family income of less than 70 percent of the BLS family budget.) | 5. Intended for most severely disadvantaged in terms of length of unemployment and prospects of obtaining a job. Consideration to be given to: Vietnam-era veterans; public assistance recipients; groups facing labor market disadvantages, identified as: offenders, persons of limited English language proficiency, handicapped, women, single parents, displaced homemakers, youth, older workers, persons lacking educational credentials, and others named by the Secretary of Labor. Equitable treatment for significant segments of the unemployed population. |
| | | VI Countercyclical public service employment | 6. Unemployed 10 of last 12 weeks, and unemployed at time of determination; and an AFDC or SSI recipient or a member of a low-income family. (Low-income is defined as a family income of less than 100 percent of the BLS lower level family budget.) | 6. The same as in 5, above. |

15 or more weeks, exhausted UI entitlement, or was an AFDC recipient. (Low-income defined as family income of less than 70 percent of the BLS lower level family budget.)

defined as family income of less than 70 percent of the BLS lower level family budget.)

structurally unemployed, targeting is more relevant than in the counter-cyclical Title VI. *In addition to disabled and Vietnam-era veterans and to public assistance recipients, who are specifically mentioned in the reauthorization act, the committee recommends that Title IID preference be given to persons of low educational attainment.*

Vietnam-era and disabled veterans are included because of overriding national policies. Consideration for public assistance recipients is consistent with policies to provide a positive alternative to transfer payments and to use CETA as an instrument of welfare reform. Priority for persons of low education is justified because that group traditionally has the poorest prospects for obtaining suitable jobs. Preference for these four categories of applicants should not foreclose selection of persons from other vulnerable groups and locally determined significant segments.

Objective Rating of Applicants   To ensure that persons hired are not only eligible but are the most in need and represent target groups proportionately, some prime sponsors have devised objective methods of rating applicants. In San Joaquin applicants are given "eligibility points" for factors such as length of unemployment, veteran status, educational attainment, and previous income. Applicants with the highest scores are placed first. This has proved a useful control over the referral and selection process and can be used to balance the proportions of eligible groups. *The committee urges the Department of Labor to promote the use of rating systems for selecting PSE candidates in an objective and equitable manner.*

Incentive System   *The* DOL *should also consider using discretionary funds for incentives to achieve targeting.* Incentives could be based on achievement of flexible norms, which would take into consideration local circumstances and be arrived at individually in consultation with prime sponsors. For example, if the goal is to hire persons with low educational attainment, discretionary funds could be used to reimburse sponsors for part of the cost of hiring such persons above the agreed-upon norm. This would enable sponsors to meet federal objectives without diminishing attention to other groups of applicants.

Job Search   As another method of ensuring that those with the least prospects of obtaining employment are hired, *the* DOL *should urge prime sponsors (or, by delegation, the employment service or other agency) to offer job search training to all enrollees prior to employment in* PSE. If all those selected for public service employment were given job search training, those with the best qualifications may be able to find suitable unsubsidized jobs directly, leaving the CETA openings for those experiencing more labor market problems.

The widespread practice of preselecting candidates by the employing agencies, which usually results in hiring of the best qualified applicants and is also susceptible to nepotism and political favoritism, should be eliminated. The use of an independent agency, not subject to local political pressures, to make referrals based on an objective rating system, would restrain this practice. Employing agencies that do not accept persons referred to them could be denied participants.

ENFORCING ELIGIBILITY RULES

Whatever effect the strict EJPEA eligibility rules might have had on improving targeting was reduced by the sizable proportion of ineligibles in public service employment programs. Difficulties in determining family income, self-certification by applicants, loose methods of verification, and, more important, the rush to enroll participants and failure to assign accountability for mispayments, all contributed to ineligibility. If eligibility was certified by the employment service, neither the prime sponsor nor the employment service was liable for repayment of CETA PSE funds paid to participants found to be ineligible. This policy encouraged the use of the employment service in the program, but it was not without its price. A Department of Labor audit in selected areas found that 12 percent of those hired under the new eligibility rules were ineligible; other sources indicate even higher rates of ineligibility.

Recommendations

The reauthorization act gives the Department of Labor more authority to enforce eligibility rules. Prime sponsors are clearly accountable for misspent funds if they fail to comply with the act. The DOL regulations interpret compliance to mean maintaining a record of the applicants' employment, welfare, family income, handicap, veteran, and school status, and other pertinent data; a review of the applicant record for completeness and internal consistency; and a follow-up check on a statistically significant sample of participants to verify data furnished by them. More thorough verification would, or course, entail more time and higher administrative costs. *The committee recommends an appropriate increase in permissible administrative costs for verification of eligibility and program monitoring.* This investment would pay off in effectiveness in reaching target populations.

Efforts to control eligibility and tighten the selection process should be high on the agenda of the independent monitoring unit to be established by each prime sponsor under the CETA reauthorization act. The DOL should develop a strategy to strengthen the integrity of the program by training the regional office staff to recognize program weaknesses and by assisting prime sponsor staff in the use of objective methods of selecting participants and other measures to prevent program abuses. Under CETA reauthorization, the auditing and compliance function of the DOL is considerably strengthened. The committee assumes that monitoring of eligibility processes will be one of the responsibilities of program monitors.

REVISING ALLOCATION FORMULAS

The committee believes that the allocation formulas do not adequately reflect the targeting objectives of the act. Although eligibility is limited to the low-income unemployed population, the Title VI allocation formula has no income element. In an earlier report the committee recommended that the Title VI formula be revised to take into account new eligibility requirements under EJPEA (National Research Council, 1978a, p. 22). Revision is even more crucial now, since the reauthorization act changes PSE eligibility standards for Title IID and Title VI by combining income with unemployment. The Title VI formula under the reauthorization act continues to distribute funds solely on the basis of unemployment; the Title IID formula includes a family income factor as well (adults in low-income families).

Recommendations

The committee recommends that consideration be given to developing a measure that combines duration of unemployment and low income (see National Commission on Employment and Unemployment Statistics, 1979). While there are difficulties in developing a measure with sufficient geographic detail, which can be updated from year to year, such a factor would more accurately channel funds to urban and rural areas where those most in need are concentrated. The income factor should be standardized for rural–urban and for regional differences; the factor used in the Title IID formula (adults in low-income families) does not have these adjustments.

Consideration might also be given to adjusting for differentials in wage levels in the public service employment formulas. An allotment of $100,000 may support 20 positions in a low-wage area but only 10 in a high-wage area. An allocation of positions rather than dollars might distribute resources more equitably.

One of the weaknesses of the Title VI allocation formula is that it permits distribution of resources to areas with tight labor markets or even labor shortages. In fiscal 1979 some 20 areas with unemployment rates below 4 percent received over $50 million in Title VI allotments. These include cities and suburban counties with unemployment rates as low as 2 percent. Judging by recent lower unemployment rates, more than 100 prime sponsor areas would probably have rates below 4 percent in the fiscal 1980 allocation. *The committee recommends that Congress revise the Title VI formula to exclude prime sponsor areas with unemployment rates of less than 4 percent from receiving Title VI funds except for any part of the allotment based on unemployment in subareas or pockets of substantial unemployment within their jurisdiction.* Trimming out areas with low unemployment is consistent with the countercyclical objectives of Title VI and avoids competition with the private sector for tight labor resources. Moreover, governments in areas with low unemployment are more likely to have adequate tax resources and are better able to provide essential services than depressed areas.

PROJECTS

EJPEA mandated the use of projects to provide new countercyclical jobs with the expectation that projects would be useful short-term activities outside the scope of regular public service employment. Whether the activities created are useful public services and whether the kinds of activities are likely to provide training and experience for participants leading to unsubsidized employment are significant issues for policymakers.

RESTRICTING SUBSTITUTION

The major reason for the project approach was to ensure that CETA public service employment would not replace locally funded public employment positions. An earlier study concluded that in the first 10 calendar quarters of the CETA public service jobs program substitution averaged 35 percent (National Research Council, 1978b, p. 179).

The present study does not deal directly with the question of substitution. However, some of the findings incidental to the study have a bearing on the subject. Field research associates, analyzing the kinds of activities being performed, the fiscal and budgetary situation of the prime sponsor, and the use of nonprofit agencies, found that, in most areas, CETA projects did generate jobs that otherwise would not have existed. However, a loose definition of projects and the prospect of recycling projects limit their effectiveness.

Recommendations

Projects would be more effective in constraining substitution if they were defined more tightly, limited to a short time span, and operated to a substantial degree by nonprofit agencies.

Project Scale and Definition In implementing EJPEA, the project definition was diluted to make it easier for prime sponsors to meet urgent hiring goals. As finally issued, the DOL regulations permit projects that are extensions of ongoing local activities rather than require new activities. While the change allows a broader range of activities, it also increases the probability of substitution. More than 40 percent of the project jobs studied appeared to be either maintenance or extensions of activities normally funded from local tax sources, and presumably more susceptible to substitution than activities clearly outside the mainstream of local government services. The original intent of constraining substitution by a narrow definition of projects was weakened, if not abandoned, in the rush to build up PSE enrollments.

While retaining the project approach, the CETA reauthorization act weakened its influence by providing that only half of the Title VI funds be used for projects, whereas under EJPEA all new Title VI participants for positions above the sustainment level were employed in projects. Moreover, the new legislation waters down the project definition so that almost any kind of activity can be construed as a "project."

Projects have disadvantages as well as advantages. They are more likely to create jobs outside regular public service and more flexible in handling large numbers of enrollees than regular PSE activities, but there is a trade-off in terms of the usefulness of work, prospects for transition to unsubsidized employment, and heavier administrative workload. On balance, the committee believes that a higher proportion of new PSE positions should be reserved for projects. *The committee recommends that the act be amended to raise the proportion of Title VI project positions to some ratio higher than 50 percent.*

In any case, projects should be defined, either in the act or in Department of Labor regulations, so as to emphasize projects that clearly represent new activities and deemphasize those that are extensions or maintenance of ongoing services. Since Title IID and part of Title VI enrollees are available for regular, nonproject PSE, projects should be reserved largely for new activities.

Duration EJPEA limited projects to 12 months on the premise that the activities undertaken would less likely be substituted for regular ongoing public services if they had time constraints. However, since recycling of projects was permitted, and most sponsors expected that projects would be renewed, the 12-month rule was believed to be only partially effective as a deterrent to substitution.

The CETA reauthorization act extends the project limit to 18 months and permits renewal for another 18 months, further weakening the project approach. A 36-month limit encourages the expectation that the project may continue indefinitely and therefore may result in deferring possible financing of the activity from local resources. *The committee recommends that only under very exceptional circumstances should a project be permitted to continue beyond 18 months, and under no circumstances beyond 36 months.* Eighteen months is also the limit for an individual's participation in PSE under the reauthorization act. Ending projects after 18 months and developing new ones will make for heavier administrative workloads and may result in dropping worthwhile projects, but this may be an acceptable price for deterring substitution. Moreover, it may serve the interests of sponsors who are leery of creating an expectation that services will continue when the PSE program is reduced or terminated.

Use of Nonprofit Organizations The conference report accompanying EJPEA urged the DOL to contract with nonprofit agencies for a substantial proportion of projects. The expectation was that these agencies would fund new activities. As a result of DOL prodding, 30 percent of project funds were allotted by local and state sponsors to a variety of community-based and other nonprofit organizations.

Local officials surveyed by field research associates viewed nonprofits as more likely than government agencies to create jobs that would not otherwise exist. They also observed that nonprofit projects frequently provided services to the low-income population. On the other hand, nonprofit organizations frequently have difficulty in supervising project participants and administering programs. Monitoring many small projects operated by diverse private agencies created administrative problems for prime sponsors.

The CETA reauthorization act does not urge the use of nonprofit organizations for projects, but it does list community-based organizations, community development groups, and other private nonprofit organizations as potential project applicants, along with governmental agencies. Moreover, the lower average wage permitted under the reauthorization act may tend to encourage use of nonprofit agencies, since their wage scales are not fixed as rigidly as government salaries. *The committee agrees with the DOL position urging prime sponsor and program agents to provide a substantial proportion of project funds to nonprofit agencies.* However, the DOL and sponsors should closely supervise the use of these funds in view of the limited administrative experience of many nonprofit organizations.

Direct Control of Substitution   The CETA reauthorization act has new controls and enforcement procedures for dealing with substitution and other program abuses, including establishing prime sponsor monitoring units and assigning responsibility to the prime sponsor for any violations of its subcontractors. However, DOL oversight of maintenance of effort is still weak. With a general lack of understanding of how to identify substitution, there is a tendency simply to respond to complaints.

The committee favors intensified auditing and other administrative measures to ensure that local governments maintain existing levels of effort and use PSE to increase the number of jobs over what otherwise would exist. Some direct administrative measures that might be considered by auditors in monitoring cases include (a) determining the base funding level of local government units that use CETA positions, allowing for cost of living increases, and auditing to see if the base level plus increments are being maintained; and (b) establishing a ratio of CETA employees to regular employees for a prime sponsor (or for an employing agency within a prime sponsor jurisdiction) and monitoring to ensure that the ratio is not exceeded in hiring replacements. While these are not definitive measures of substitution, they do identify situations that need further examination.

In addition, the DOL should study ways of identifying and dealing with more subtle forms of substitution such as failure to budget for needed increases in staff in anticipation of the availability of CETA workers. *The committee recommends that the DOL establish uniform definitions and concepts of the various kinds of substitution and authorize a study for developing professional standards and methods of analysis and auditing.* With public service employment likely to become a permanent feature of manpower programs, it would appear to be cost-effective to invest in developing and installing systematic methods of dealing with this problem.

QUALITY OF PROJECTS

One of the issues in public service employment is the quality of the jobs. The committee study found that nearly all Title VI projects do provide useful public service, although the quality of projects was somewhat affected by short deadlines: One-third were considered high priority services.

Although project activities were considered useful, the programs gave scant attention to training and experience that would help workers prepare for unsubsidized jobs in the public or private sector. Attention was on the more immediate goal of rapid hiring.

Most of the jobs in government agencies involved blue-collar or unskilled labor. More than half of project employees were engaged in public works and parks and recreation activities, and approximately 40 percent of the positions were for laborers. Projects in nonprofit organizations, on the other hand, were heavily concentrated in social services and improvement of low-income housing. These called for relatively high proportions of professional and skilled workers.

Much of the public works and parks activity was outdoor cleanup and maintenance. This kind of work had little counterpart in the competitive job market. Moreover, these jobs were customarily filled by men, which limited opportunities for AFDC recipients and other women. The committee sees a need for designing projects that will provide the participants with the kind of experience that will improve their opportunities for employment in unsubsidized jobs.

Recommendations

The CETA reauthorization act recognized that project jobs frequently do not contribute to employability development. Because PSE enrollees are to be drawn increasingly from the long-term unemployed and from low-income and welfare households, the act requires that the sponsor must assess the employability of each participant, and provide employment counseling, training, or other services wherever necessary. Ten percent of the Title VI allotted funds in fiscal 1979 and 5 percent thereafter must be used for this purpose.

The committee recommends that the prime sponsors develop PSE projects that combine employability services and training with PSE to provide skills and experience transferable to public or private employment. This requires sufficient lead time for the planning, review, and selection of projects that meet these aims. Hurried implementation should not take precedence over careful preparation, execution, and monitoring of projects. *The committee also recommends that the 10 percent of allotted funds received for training under Title VI be continued.* The reauthorization act provides for only 5 percent for years subsequent to fiscal 1979.

Transition Potential Placement rates in PSE programs have been relatively low. In fiscal 1978, only 31 percent of those who terminated from Title VI entered jobs, compared with 38 percent of Title II terminees and 45 percent for those leaving Title I. The amount of emphasis to be placed on transition to unsubsidized jobs is fuzzy in the CETA reauthorization act. Although the purpose of Title IID is to enable participants to move into nonsubsidized employment, the intent of Title VI is merely "to provide temporary employment during periods of high unemployment." The difference is apparently intentional. The Senate version of Title VI stressed transition but the House version did not—and the House prevailed.

The committee study found that the neglect of transition in Title VI projects was due to the Department of Labor emphasis on rapid hiring as well as to the lack of emphasis in the legislation itself. Practices related to the absorption of participants into regular public service jobs or transfer into private employment were deferred until the end of the project cycle.

The framers of the CETA reauthorization act provided that some of the Title VI as well as Title II administrative funds could be used for training or counseling to prepare participants for transition based on an assessment of each participant's employability. Restricting the duration of tenure to 18 months may create a greater sense of urgency for transition efforts, but the targeting provisions may make it harder to find suitable nonsubsidized jobs for a more disadvantaged clientele.

The committee believes that neither the act nor the Department of Labor regulations convey to prime sponsors a serious commitment to this objective, particularly for Title VI. *The committee recommends that greater emphasis be placed on job search and placement for Title VI and Title IID participants.* At a minimum prime sponsors should be required to develop employability plans for each Title VI as well as each Title IID participant. Arrangements should be made for coordinated efforts with employment service agencies for job search and referral to suitable openings before termination of the client's PSE enrollment.

PROCESSING PROJECTS

About 85,000 projects were reviewed by local officials, planning staffs, and councils in the first 6 months of the PSE buildup. The average project had six enrollees; 23 percent had only one. This generated an enormous workload for CETA staff and planning councils as well as increased responsibility for supervision and monitoring. Where program agents or subjurisdictions were involved there were several additional layers of clearance.

Recommendations

Administration of the project approach is far more complex than that of other public service employment programs. *The committee recommends that only projects employing three or more persons be funded in order to reduce the development and review workload.* Smaller projects should be handled as individual positions under regular PSE programs. This would eliminate 40 percent of the projects but would have only a small effect on the number of project participants.

The cutback in allowable administrative costs to 10 percent for Title VI in fiscal 1979 (which returns to 15 percent thereafter) could cause problems for areas for which the expenditure level, divided between the prime sponsor and project operators, might restrict the kinds of projects that could be undertaken. Nonprofit project operators who could not afford to pay for supervision and overhead for a small number of enrollees would be particularly affected. However, since average administrative costs have not exceeded 8 percent in the past and since extra funds are provided for training, *the committee recommends that the administrative cost limit in the act remain unchanged except for an additional allowance for verification of eligibles and for monitoring, as previously discussed.* Exceptions could be made administratively for hardship cases as long as the average remains below statutory limits.

The role of the planning council in project review needs to be reassessed. In the rapid buildup of projects under the economic expansion, project review was often perfunctory. Nonetheless, the principle of grass roots participation is sound. With a more orderly program and with fewer new projects, council review can be meaningful, and it is a worthwhile check on the kinds of projects developed. The CETA reauthorization act does not specifically require approval of each project by local planning councils, and the DOL regulations call for only review and comment. *The committee recommends a more positive role for the planning council. At a minimum the council should be responsible for recommending guidelines and criteria for choosing projects.*

PSE WAGE RATES

The wage provisions for PSE were not changed by the 1976 revision of CETA. PSE jobs were required to pay the "prevailing wage" for similar work in the same agency. Wages from CETA funds could average no more than $7,800 for the country as a whole, and the maximum CETA wage was set at $10,000. However, local agencies could supplement CETA wages by any amount from their own funds. In 1977, the median wage for project jobs was under $7,700, including supplementation.

The wage provisions did not hinder the PSE expansion in most areas. Half of the areas reported an ample supply of applicants with a wide range of skills willing to take project jobs at $10,000 or less. But a quarter of the areas found it was difficult to hire supervisors and others with special skills. Some sponsors supplemented CETA wages to fill positions calling for more skilled workers. Others, to stay within wage limits, developed jobs for less skilled persons.

The 1978 reauthorization lowered the average wage that could be paid and limited supplementation. This change reflected uneasiness over the fact that many PSE participants whose wages were supplemented by local governments were earning more than their counterparts in private industry—a development inconsistent with the objective of providing emergency jobs for the low-income unemployed. The reauthorization act reduced the allowable average wage from $7,800 to $7,200 in 1979 and limited supplementation of Title VI wages to 10 percent of the maximum wage for each area (no supplementation is permitted for Title II). Flexibility was provided for high-wage areas by allowing the maximum CETA wage to go as much as 20 percent above $10,000. Both the $7,200 average and the maximum are adjusted for each prime sponsor by the relation of area wages to the national average. The wage adjustments were originally based on unemployment insurance employer reports and did not necessarily reflect differentials in government wages.

Lower wages are intended to have three effects: (a) to discourage applications from persons who have alternative employment opportunities, thus focusing on those who are more disadvantaged; (b) to make substitution less likely; and (c) to discourage participants from remaining in CETA positions if they have opportunities for unsubsidized employment. However, there may be several difficulties. Sponsors with high prevailing wages may find it hard to locate positions in which low wage PSE workers may be used. This may lead to greater use of nonprofit organizations where the prevailing wage problem is less severe. Moreover, targeted clientele groups such as public assistance and unemployment insurance recipients may have less incentive to accept PSE jobs. Wage restraints will be reflected in the kinds of projects and activities that can be undertaken. There may be a shift to projects that are viewed as having less utility than those presently undertaken.

The lower average PSE wage and the limit on supplementation could have their sharpest effects in northern and western cities where starting wages for many unskilled government jobs may exceed the CETA average, and some even exceed the CETA maximum despite the regional wage differentials permitted.

Recommendations

The committee believes that the wage structure introduced under the CETA reauthorization act, which also provides for annual adjustments related to the Consumer Price Index, is consistent with the targeting, maintenance of effort, and transition objectives of the legislation. However, the technique used for adjusting the average and the maximum wage among areas does not allow a wide enough range of permissible wages to accommodate high wage areas. *The committee recommends that the DOL continue to refine the geographic wage adjustment techniques to establish wage standards related to the needs of high- as well as low-wage areas.* This can be done by using public sector as well as private industry wages as a basis for arriving at specific area wage differentials and by using rates for discrete cities or counties or SMSAs, whichever is higher. The committee also recommends that the effects of wages on program operations be monitored closely so that Congress can be alerted to the impact of a lower wage on the program.

ADMINISTRATION OF PUBLIC SERVICE EMPLOYMENT PROGRAMS

FEDERAL ADMINISTRATION

Between January 1977, when President Carter announced the economic stimulus package, and May 1977, when the appropriations act was passed, the Department of Labor took a number of steps to prepare for a rapid buildup of enrollment. It established national employment goals and required local sponsors to set up hiring schedules. It instructed prime sponsors and local employment service offices to cooperate in identifying and screening Title VI applicants eligible under the new rules established by EJPEA. It directed sponsors to develop a list of projects for funding under Title VI and urged them to involve private nonprofit organizations as well as local government agencies.

In its haste to build up enrollments to meet the economic stimulus goals, the Department of Labor modified the program design. Regulations drafted after the enactment of EJPEA in October 1976 were revised several times before issuance in May 1977. The definitions of projects and eligibility standards were relaxed. Most important, the Department of Labor absolved sponsors from liability for ineligible participants if they made appropriate arrangements with employment service offices for verification of the unemployment, welfare, and family income status of enrollees.

Under continuous pressure from the department, hiring goals were met, but with some sacrifice of other objectives. The emphasis was on "body counts," not on who was enrolled, nor the quality of projects. Job development and placement received scant attention. The history of manpower programs is replete with similar examples of trading short-term goals for long-term program objectives.

Recommendations

The 4-year extension of CETA, through fiscal 1982 under the reauthorization act, offers an opportunity for more stable administration. *The committee recommends that appropriation and allocation of funds be made far enough in advance to allow sufficient lead time for planning, development, and communication of procedures, technical assistance, and training of staff at all levels of government.* The act does permit appropriations a year in advance for all titles of CETA to afford adequate notice, but this special procedure has only been used for the Economic Stimulus Appropriations Act. Utilizing this 2-year provision for Title IID funds would contribute to more orderly management. Title VI appropriations, intended to be tied to unemployment levels, would of necessity continue to be made annually.

The CETA reauthorization act continues the trend back toward greater federal control. The original principle of local control over decategorized programs has been deemphasized, with each amendment adding special programs for special purposes, e.g., public service employment and youth employment programs. Under the reauthorization act, several more categorical programs were introduced, including skill upgrading and a separate title (Title VII) for private sector initiatives.

State and local governments are becoming brokers, handling earmarked federal funds. This places a greater burden on the federal establishment for technical assistance and guidance. However, regional offices are not always able to provide the kind of help needed in such technical areas as management information systems, accounting procedures, and job matching systems. *The committee sees a need for more specialized technical assistance with emphasis on improvement of systems as well as on program content.* Where necessary, outside consultants should be used for highly technical, nonrecurring activities, such as training in new systems.

The committee stresses the importance of separating federal monitoring functions from technical assistance. Under present regional office procedures, both of these functions are performed by the same federal officials.

This introduces a compliance relationship that could impair the effectiveness of the regional office representative in providing technical assistance.

LOCAL ADMINISTRATION

Administrative processes for public service employment projects are more complex than those for nonproject PSE programs. Staffing, contract supervision, dealing with merit systems and retirement funds, maintaining pools of eligibles, and developing suitable projects were some of the difficult areas. And the expansion of the project program coincided with youth legislation and other new initiatives. Increasingly, CETA is becoming a patchwork of categorical programs with different eligibility requirements.

There are signs that the size of the CETA organization is approaching that of older human resources institutions such as the employment service, unemployment insurance service, and welfare agencies. The CETA staff engaged in administrative and management functions in local areas and states has grown sharply from 20,000 to 33,000 between 1976 and 1978, and the ratio of administrative to total PSE expenditures nearly doubled from 3.7 to 7.2 percent between fiscal 1976 and fiscal 1978. The 33,000 positions do not include employees engaged in providing direct services or PSE enrollees assigned to administrative positions.

The CETA reauthorization act intended to streamline the grant application system and reduce the frequency of submission of plans. This may cut down paperwork. On the other hand, the legislation introduced new programs with detailed specifications.

In planning the PSE buildup, the Department of Labor urged prime sponsor and employment service agencies to screen AFDC recipients, unemployment insurance beneficiaries, UI exhaustees, and other low-income, long-term unemployed and establish a pool of eligibles that could be drawn upon to fill the new PSE slots. This mechanism was useful initially, but pools proved to be difficult to maintain because of divided responsibility, communication gaps, and the changing status of pool members. In addition, many applicants did not enter through the pool.

Recommendations

Nevertheless, the committee believes that each prime sponsor should maintain its own active file of eligible applicants for PSE and other CETA programs as a means of applying objective criteria in selection and referral of applicants. Applicants could be ranked by a weighting system that takes into account target groups and priorities identified in the act as well as those determined locally (see page 22). The file itself, continuously updated, could be a source of data for determining the proportions of various groups in the eligible labor force.

RELATIONS WITH EMPLOYMENT SERVICE AND OTHER INSTITUTIONS

Under EJPEA, there were incentives for both prime sponsors and the employment service to cooperate in determining eligibility. For sponsors, there was immunity for mispayments to ineligibles, while the employment service received placement credit for referrals to PSE slots. Nearly all sponsors entered into agreements with the employment service for verifying eligibility. The importance of this to the employment service system is reflected in placement data. In fiscal 1978, one-eighth of the individuals placed by the employment service agencies were PSE referrals.

Working together had mixed results, however. There was often duplication in verifying eligibility, and the applicant pool system started to fall apart as soon as hiring goals were reached. On the whole, however, relationships improved; there is more agreement that the employment service has a limited role in intake for PSE as well as for Title I programs. There is clearly a potential for greater cooperation in job search prior to assignment of enrollees to public service employment (see p. 22) and in placement activities on termination of enrollment. However, the existence of two national manpower systems with an undefined relationship continues to be troublesome. The CETA reauthorization act requires only that employment security agencies be informed of PSE openings so that they can notify unemployment insurance recipients and other applicants. DOL regulations require a written agreement with state employment security agencies. In a previous report, the committee recommended that an independent study be conducted of the employment service–CETA relationship as a basis for conclusions on the appropriate accommodation of the two manpower systems.

The current study noted the lack of linkage between CETA and other agencies in the community that could provide supportive services for participants. The main concern of sponsors was to get participants on board, not to provide them with support services. The potential leverage of stationing PSE participants in nonprofit agencies in exchange for reciprocal services is not being used mainly because of administrative difficulties in trying to establish cooperative arrangements among agencies with various eligibility rules and procedures. At a minimum there should be more coordination among the CETA programs themselves. *The committee recommends that the DOL more actively promote cooperative arrangements among CETA titles and between CETA and other agencies and that local elected officials use their authority to bring related human resources programs closer together.* PSE should be viewed as a component of a broad effort to enhance the employability of the disadvantaged and to improve opportunities.

3 Department of Labor Implementation

The Emergency Jobs Program Extension Act of 1976, followed by the Economic Stimulus Appropriations Act of 1977, changed the substance and the scale of the temporary public service employment programs under CETA. The major PSE program, Title VI, which was originally designed as a countercyclical measure, was revised to limit eligibility for most new jobs to the low-income, long-term unemployed and to require that new public service jobs be in short-duration projects rather than in regular public services. Implementing these major changes while expanding the program required forceful administrative measures at federal and local levels. This chapter reviews the steps taken by the Department of Labor to carry out the major program changes and to double the size of the PSE programs. It also describes the problems encountered in trying to accomplish both objectives very quickly.

EARLY PUBLIC SERVICE EMPLOYMENT PROGRAMS

The Comprehensive Employment and Training Act of December 1973 was enacted as a block grant program to decentralize manpower programs and to give local officials flexibility in choosing programs and services for their areas. The public service employment component of CETA (Title II) was a minor element (one-sixth of total funds appropriated in the first year) limited to areas of substantial unemployment (6.5 percent). The $400 million authorized under Title II for fiscal 1975 was enough to support a program of only 50,000 enrollees.

38

As unemployment rose, public service employment became a more important element of manpower policy. In December 1974 Congress passed the Emergency Jobs and Unemployment Assistance Act (EJUAA), which established Title VI, a program to create jobs in the public sector for the unemployed. Two-and-a-half billion dollars was authorized to support 300,000 positions for 1 year. Unlike Title II, Title VI was not limited to areas of substantial unemployment; most prime sponsor areas were experiencing high unemployment, and the two programs were virtually indistinguishable.

With the implementation of Title VI, PSE grew from 53,000 enrollees in September 1974 to 370,000 by early 1976 (Table 2).[1] PSE participants made up a significant proportion of state and local government employment, rising from less than 1 percent in December 1974 to 2.7 percent a year and a half later.[2] Under the Emergency Jobs Programs Extension Act the proportion was to reach close to 6 percent by the end of fiscal 1978, as shown in Table 3.

In Congress and in the administration, however, there was growing disillusionment about the effectiveness of the temporary employment program as a countercyclical measure. First, the tendency of local governments to substitute federal for local funds partly offset the effect of job creation. One study found substitution averaging 35 percent in the first 10 quarters, from June 1974 through December 1976 (National Research Council, 1978b, pp. 178–80).[3] Second, adults in PSE programs were generally white men, of prime working age, better educated and less disadvantaged than those in the employability development programs of Title I. Third, the lack of emphasis on transition of enrollees to unsubsidized jobs resulted in a poor placement record. In 1976, when EJPEA was passed, fewer than one in four of the individuals who terminated from PSE programs entered unsubsidized employment; the ratio in Title I programs was one in three.[4]

[1] The 53,000 includes some carryover enrollees under the Emergency Employment Act (PEP program). In June 1974 Congress appropriated $250 million to continue the PEP program for about 9 months into fiscal 1975.

[2] Includes CETA positions contracted to nonprofit organizations, estimated to have been about 15 percent in fiscal 1977 and 30 percent in projects after the expansion.

[3] See also National Commission for Employment Policy (1978a). The latter study, based on observations in selected areas, concluded that the displacement rate in July 1977, 2 months after the beginning of the expansion under the Economic Stimulus Appropriations Act of 1977, was 18 percent.

[4] The job entry rate for Title VI, as reported by the Department of Labor, rose from 27 percent in fiscal 1976 to 34 percent in fiscal 1977 after EJPEA went into effect and to 31 percent in fiscal 1978. Rates for Title II were: 17 percent in fiscal 1976, 18 percent in fiscal 1977, and 38 percent in fiscal 1978.

TABLE 2 Public Service Employment Participants Under the Emergency Employment Act and CETA Compared with the Number of Unemployed, September 1971-June 1978 (thousands)

Year and Month[a]	Unemployed (seas. adj.)			Unemployment Rate (percent)	PSE Participants[b]	PSE Participants as Percent of Unemployed
	0-14 Weeks	15 Weeks or More	Total			
1971 September	3,858	1,238	5,096	6.0	12	0.2
December	3,831	1,286	5,117	6.0	83	1.6
1972 March	3,702	1,223	4,925	5.8	136	2.8
June	3,731	1,131	4,861	5.6	169	3.5
September	3,718	1,123	4,841	5.6	154	3.2
December	3,430	999	4,429	5.1	138	3.1
1973 March	3,434	877	4,311	4.9	131	3.0
June	3,526	763	4,289	4.8	118	2.8
September	3,507	770	4,277	4.8	106	2.5
December	3,590	754	4,344	4.9	84	1.9
1974 March	3,757	834	4,591	5.0	61	1.3
June	3,953	903	4,856	5.3	43	0.9
September	4,347	1,001	5,348	5.9	53	1.0
December	5,213	1,326	6,539	7.2	103	1.6

	5,319	2,777	8,096	8.7	311	3.8
June	5,319	2,777	8,096	8.7	311	3.8
September	5,181	2,884	8,065	8.5	332	4.1
December	4,878	2,931	7,809	8.2	353	4.5
1976 March	4,532	2,412	6,944	7.6	369	5.3
June	4,978	2,236	7,214	7.5	323	4.5
September	5,186	2,272	7,458	7.7	305	4.1
December	5,141	2,462	7,603	7.8	284	3.7
1977 March	5,084	2,008	7,092	7.4	318	4.5
June	5,126	1,788	6,914	7.1	376	5.4
September	4,936	1,834	6,770	6.8	553	8.2
December	4,565	1,797	6,362	6.4	637	10.0
1978 March	4,685	1,463	6,148	6.2	739	12.0
June	4,523	1,231	5,754	5.7	722	12.6

SOURCE: Bureau of Labor Statistics and Employment and Training Administration, U.S. Department of Labor.

[a] CETA became effective in July 1974; the Emergency Jobs and Unemployment Assistance Act of 1974 in January 1975; the Emergency Jobs Programs Extension Act in October 1976; and the Economic Stimulus Appropriations Act in May 1977.
[b] Includes participants under Titles I, II, and VI of CETA and under the Emergency Employment Act.

TABLE 3   CETA Public Service Employment Participants as a Proportion of Total State and Local Government Employment

Month and Year	State and Local Goverment Employment[a] (thousands)	CETA Public Service Employment Participants[b] (thousands)	Percent of Total
December 1974	11,677	103	0.9
June 1975	11,934	311	2.6
June 1976	12,125	323	2.7
September 1977	12,479	553	4.4
September 1978	12,693	722	5.7

SOURCE: Bureau of Labor Statistics and Employment and Training Administration, U.S. Department of Labor.

[a] Seasonally adjusted. Figures include PSE employment.

[b] Not adjusted to exclude CETA PSE participants assigned to private nonprofit agencies.

EJPEA REFORMS

The Emergency Jobs Programs Extension Act of 1976, which extended Title VI for 1 year, attempted to deal with two of these problems—targeting and substitution. To increase the participation of disadvantaged persons, EJPEA required that all new hires above the June 1976 level (plus half of those needed to sustain that level) must be low-income, long-term unemployed persons or welfare recipients. Congress was also concerned with the mounting costs of unemployment insurance. The duration of supplemental benefits had been extended, and the combined state and federal outlays reached record levels of over $18 billion in the fiscal year ending June 1976. To check the growing burden of UI, Congress directed that a share of new project jobs be reserved for unemployment insurance beneficiaries as well as those who exhausted entitlement for benefits in proportion to their numbers in the eligible population.

To discourage substitution, the new legislation required that all new public service jobs above the sustainment level be in "projects" that could not exceed 12 months.[5] Moreover, the conference report accompanying the act stated that prime sponsors were expected to provide a substantial portion of project funds (later defined by ETA as one-third) to nonprofit agencies to assure that new jobs were in fact created.

EJPEA was passed in the waning days of the Ford administration, which supported the changes and the extension of Title VI through fiscal year

[5]The sustainment level for each prime sponsor is the number of Title VI PSE employees in June 1976 or October 1976, whichever is higher.

1977 but did not seek an increase in the program level. Unemployment had fallen from a peak rate of close to 9 percent in the spring of 1975 to 7.7 percent by the fall of 1976 and was expected to continue to decline as the momentum of recovery picked up. In the face of these developments, the administration policy was to shrink the size of the Title VI program. Funds for Title VI were not included in the original budget for fiscal 1978, but the administration requested and Congress approved a continuing resolution authorizing $1.38 billion, the amount necessary to phase out Title VI completely by September 1977. In October 1976, shortly after EJPEA passed, the Department of Labor advised prime sponsors to phase down PSE employment by attrition, transferring enrollees to Title II, finding permanent jobs, or simply terminating the excess number of participants in order to stay within allotted funds. Under the circumstances, the DOL expected the principal provisions of EJPEA to have only marginal, if any, effect.

THE ECONOMIC STIMULUS APPROPRIATIONS ACT

The change in administration brought a new emphasis on public service employment programs. In January 1977, President Carter proposed a multibillion-dollar program to stimulate the economy and to lower the unemployment rate, which had hovered around 8 percent throughout 1976 and showed no signs of declining. In fact, the unemployment rate had edged up from 7.5 percent in June to 7.8 percent in December. The administration was particularly concerned with the very high unemployment among minorities, veterans, and youth. The economic stimulus package included measures to revive the economy generally, as well as programs for disadvantaged groups.

The Economic Stimulus Appropriations Act provided $20.0 billion in supplemental 1977 funds—$5 billion for general revenue sharing, $1 billion for antirecessionary revenue sharing, $4 billion for local public works, and lesser amounts for other purposes. The largest sum, $9.4 billion, went to the Employment and Training Administration to expand public service employment, initiate new youth and veterans programs, and to experiment with improved training programs (Table 4).

The 2-year $8 billion appropriation for Titles II and VI for fiscal 1977 and 1978 was an increase of $6.6 billion over the amount previously authorized by the continuing resolution for 1 year (Table 5). Federal officials believed that the rapid buildup of public service jobs was essential to maximize the effect of the stimulus strategy. From a level of about 300,000 participants in early 1977 they projected an increase to 725,000 by the following December (later revised to March 1978). This was expected

TABLE 4   Employment and Training Administration
Funds Under the Economic Stimulus Appropriations Act,
Fiscal 1977 (millions of dollars)

Program	Amount
TOTAL	9,429.4
Public service employment	7,987.0
Title II	1,140.0
Title VI	6,847.0
Youth programs	1,000.0
Job Corps	68.0
Skill Training Improvement Program (STIP)	250.0
Help through Industry Retraining and Employment (HIRE)	120.0
Program administration (salaries and expenses)	4.4

SOURCE: Employment and Training Report of the President, 1978.

to reduce unemployment directly and stimulate demand for goods and services.

Under the enlarged PSE program, the EJPEA reforms for clientele targeting and the use of projects assumed much greater importance. The planning for welfare reform that was going on at the time added further significance to the Title VI expansion. The Labor Department was advocating a large employment program as part of a new welfare system, while supporters of a minimum guaranteed income were arguing that not enough useful jobs appropriate to the skills of the nation's poor could be created. Successful implementation of a large Title VI program targeted to low-income individuals would bolster the department's position and was repeatedly cited as evidence of the feasibility of temporary public service jobs.

ETA RESPONSE

Momentum for the PSE expansion began as the Carter administration prepared to take office, and Department of Labor officials were quick to act when the president officially announced the program. In January 1977, the Employment and Training Administration instructed prime sponsors to develop lists of projects and to arrange with local employment service offices to set up pools of potentially eligible unemployment insurance and welfare applicants. Regulations and instructions for grant applications issued in March and April laid the groundwork for the expansion. They

TABLE 5 CETA Appropriations, Fiscal 1974-1978 (millions of dollars)

Title	Fiscal 1974[a]	Fiscal 1975	Fiscal 1976		Fiscal 1977		Fiscal 1978
			July 1975-June 1976	July-Sept. 1976	Initial	Final	
TOTAL	2,265.6	3,742.8	5,741.8	597.6	4,695.8	8,052.8	8,061.9
I	1,010.0	1,580.0	1,580.0	395.4	1,880.0	1,880.0	1,880.0
II	370.0	400.0	1,600.0[b]	100.0	400.0	524.0	1,016.0[d]
III	180.0	239.4	268.4	58.4	239.3	1,600.7[c]	387.9
IV	150.0	175.0	140.0	43.8	197.5	274.1	417.0
VI	250.0	875.0	1,625.0	—	1,384.0	3,179.0	3,668.0[d]
Summer youth	305.6	473.4	528.4	—	595.0	595.0	693.0

SOURCE: Employment and Training Administration, U.S. Department of Labor.

[a] Appropriations for Department of Labor manpower programs corresponding with Titles I and II of CETA, and for the Emergency Employment Act corresponding with Title VI.

[b] $1,200 million authorized under Title II for both Titles II and VI.

[c] Includes $233.3 million for Young Adult Conservation Corps, Title VIII of CETA; also funds for veterans programs (HIRE), skill training improvement (STIP), and other youth programs.

[d] Forward funded from 1977 appropriation under the Economic Stimulus Appropriations Act.

TABLE 6   Planned and Actual Participants, CETA Titles II and VI, May 1977-March 1978 (thousands)

Date	Titles II and VI Planned	Actual	Title VI Planned	Actual	Title II Planned	Actual
1977						
May 13	—	298	—	245	—	53
July 1	328	361	267	295	62	66
September 30	507	533	422	440	85	93
December 30	664	615	555	506	109	109
1978						
March 3	725	742	600	613	125	129

SOURCE: Employment and Training Administration, U.S. Department of Labor.

required sponsors to develop projects, set hiring schedules, and establish processes for screening and selecting eligible job applicants. Employment service offices, which are also in the purview of the Employment and Training Administration, were directed to begin screening unemployment insurance claimants and enrollees in the Work Incentive Program (WIN) to identify a ready reserve of eligible applicants. The DOL urged prime sponsors to involve nonprofit organizations in projects to expand the potential for useful employment in services not otherwise available. The administration was particularly committed to hiring veterans, and a goal of 35 percent of new hires was announced in May 1977.

The appropriation act was not signed until May 13, 1977, and this delayed the timetable for the PSE expansion. Initially, ETA had planned to add 45,000 jobs a month for the first 3 months, 35,000 monthly for the second 3, and 33,000 each of the final 3 months. The national schedule was revised to stretch out the buildup, but regional offices continued to urge prime sponsors to plan according to the original schedule. Hence, during the early months, PSE employment stayed well ahead of the national plan. ETA regional offices required weekly reports from sponsors and threatened to withdraw funds from lagging sponsors. In one instance, a taped interview with a regional official explaining that several local governments were in jeopardy of losing federal "job funds" because of the lethargic response of local officials was broadcast hourly. As a result of prodding, the final goal of 725,000 by March 1 was met and surpassed (Table 6).

Although relentless pressure on national and local staffs succeeded in terms of program scale, the concomitant sacrifice in terms of program design and substantive objectives was considerable. The targeting objectives of EJPEA were only partially met, and many of the projects left open the door for substitution of federal for local resources (see discussion in Chapters 5 and 7).

REGULATIONS RELAXED

The Employment and Training Administration acted quickly to issue regulations for implementing EJPEA. Proposed regulations were published on October 26, 1976—less than 4 weeks after the act was passed. They were issued in final form on January 11, 1977, but modified on May 13, when President Carter signed the Economic Stimulus Appropriations Act.

The May 13 regulations relaxed earlier requirements. Regulations relating to project definitions, eligibility criteria, and responsibility for determining eligiblity were changed to accommodate objections of prime sponsors, speed implementation, and make administration easier. But these changes tended to frustrate the basic targeting and maintenance of effort objectives of EJPEA. Dilution of the definition of a project permitted the use of some funds for regular public service activities, making it more difficult to constrain the substitution of federal for local funds. Loosening the unemployment eligiblity standard permitted selection of persons who had been jobless intermittently but could not meet the more rigorous test of having been unemployed continuously for 15 weeks. Changing the rules for determining eligiblity reduced the liability of prime sponsors for ineligible participants increased the likelihood of enrollment of such persons. The major changes made in regulations were:

1. *Project Definition.* The January 1977 regulations, issued prior to the announcement of the economic stimulus program, defined a project as a task that provides a public service and that does not expand an existing ongoing service provided by the state, county, or municipality. The intent of Congress in requiring projects to be distinct and separate activities was to restrict the opportunity to use CETA funds for regular ongoing public service activities that otherwise would be supported by local resources. This definition limited activities under Title VI to new or one-shot activities and was strongly opposed by prime sponsors. To speed up PSE hiring, ETA adopted a looser regulation without the prohibition on expansion of ongoing services. Under the new definition, a project is a task that can be completed within 1 year, has a public service objective, will result in a specific product, and would not have been done with the applicant's existing funds.

2. *Eligibility Criteria.* The original Department of Labor regulations issued under EJPEA in January 1977 required that an applicant, besides

being from a low-income family, must have been unemployed for 15 weeks or more. Sponsors objected that this tended to eliminate deserving applicants whose spell of unemployment was interrupted. The rule was modified so that an applicant unemployed for 15 of the last 20 weeks could be eligible.

3. *Eligibility Determination.* Initially, ETA held the prime sponsor accountable for a participant's eligibility and liable for payments to persons found to be ineligible. The early regulations encouraged sponsors to seek the assistance of both the local employment service and the local welfare agency to recruit and determine the eligibility of participants, but left to the sponsors the decision whether to verify eligibility and the method of verification. Prime sponsors were troubled by the financial liability implications of the regulations and the prospect of intensive eligibility screening of job applicants with the attendant delays in hiring. In recognition of the sponsors' concerns, but chiefly to facilitate hiring, the May 1977 regulations loosened the certification requirement in two ways. First, sponsors were permitted to enroll applicants on their own certification pending verification of eligibility. If a participant was found to be ineligible within 60 days, the sponsor was not liable for repayment of wages during that period. Moreover, if the sponsor had an arrangement with the employment service or welfare agency to verify participant eligibility, the sponsor was not liable for any costs resulting from such arrangements. In short, the prime sponsor was financially liable for wage payments made to ineligible participants only if the eligibility determination was made by the prime sponsor's staff. No one was financially liable if the determination was made by the employment service.

This change in regulations had the intended effect of increasing the role of the employment service in PSE recruitment. But it did not ensure accountability for improper enrollment of PSE participants. A departmental audit, based on a small sample of sponsors, questioned the eligibility of one in eight Title VI workers and attributed the high rate of ineligibility to the practice of relying on statements made by applicants with little verification of their accuracy.

To summarize, the Employment and Training Administration responded promptly to the call for expansion of public service employment. Regulations were revised to facilitate implementation, buildup schedules were developed, prime sponsors arranged with employment service agencies to set up pools of eligible persons, and the process of choosing projects began even before the Economic Stimulus Act was passed in May 1977. Despite many problems, the goal of adding 425,000 new enrollees in 9 months was achieved. More fundamentally, the design changes envisioned by EJPEA were incorporated in the system, but modifications in the interests of speed and expediency blunted the intent of the legislation.

While the administrative goal of expanding public service employment programs was achieved, a more fundamental question is the extent to which that expansion contributed to the alleviation of unemployment. The U.S. unemployment rate began to decline before the Economic Stimulus Appropriations Act was implemented (Table 2). The number of unemployed fell by a half million in the first quarter of calendar 1977 and the rate declined from 7.8 percent to 7.4 percent. As the buildup of CETA public service employment progressed over the next 4 calendar quarters to March 1978, the rate continued to slide to 6.2 percent. While 425,000 were added to the PSE rolls, total employment increased by 3.7 million and the number of unemployed declined by nearly 1 million. CETA public service enrollees, who were 4.5 percent of total unemployed in March 1977, amounted to 12 percent a year later.[6]

Most economists acknowledge that jobs created under a public service employment program have a multiplier effect; for every newly created position, more than one additional job results from the ripple effect of increased demand. (The stimulus effect is mitigated if there is some substitution for jobs that would have existed without CETA.) However, federal outlays for public service jobs programs in 1977 were only one of a number of expansionary measures taken at that time. Increased grants for public works and antirecessionary revenue sharing were helping to accelerate state and local government expenditures. The year was also marked by growth in the private sector, particularly in manufacturing and in contract construction. The extent to which PSE contributed in stimulating aggregate demand must be weighed in relation to other forces at work in the economy. In any case, public service employment programs have unique advantages as countercyclical measures. They yield social and economic benefits, such as affording useful work experience to the less advantaged unemployed, thereby reducing inflationary pressure on wages and providing a positive alternative to transfer payments (see National Commission for Employment Policy, 1978b).

[6]Although unemployed prior to entry, CETA PSE enrollees are counted as employed in official labor force statistics while working.

4 Planning and Administration

The major design changes brought about by the Emergency Jobs Programs Extension Act and the doubling of the size of the PSE program left their mark on the planning, administration, and operation of local CETA programs.

The early emphasis of CETA was on the employability development activities of Title I—training and work experience. With the introduction of Title VI in 1975, program emphasis began to shift to creating jobs in the public sector, and this was reinforced by the PSE expansion of 1977. Local concern with the fiscal and resource implications of large-scale supplementation of local public services has, in many areas, overshadowed interest in Title I activities.

EJPEA and the expansion of PSE have introduced more complexities and rigidities into CETA. The original emphasis on encouraging broad local discretion in identifying manpower needs and developing appropriate responses is gradually being weakened as more and more of CETA funds are earmarked for prescribed uses. Moreover, it seems likely that the recategorization trend will continue, with Congress responding to each problem with a specific program. Increasingly, CETA resembles a conglomerate of special-purpose programs rather than a block grant. Although the funds available for Title I, the only decategorized title, were greater in fiscal 1978 ($1,880 million) than in fiscal 1975 ($1,580 million), they constituted only 23 percent of all CETA funds, compared with 42 percent in 1975.

Following the passage of EJPEA, there were three distinct types of PSE programs—Title VI projects, Title VI "sustainment" (regular, largely nonproject public sector employment), and Title II programs—each with its own rules of eligibility and kinds of activities. EJPEA and the PSE expansion came after nearly 3 years of experience with CETA, when most prime sponsors had consolidated their organizations and administrative procedures. But the time and scale demands of Title II and Title VI in 1977, in conjunction with several major new programs, placed new strains on the administrative structure.

This chapter examines:

1. How prime sponsors managed the expanded PSE program in addition to their other CETA responsibilities.
2. How the concentration on public service employment projects affected planning and decision-making patterns at the local level.
3. What effect the PSE expansion had on the original objectives of CETA to decentralize and decategorize manpower programs, including relationships between federal and local officials.

LITTLE BASIC CHANGE

Local planning and grass roots participation were among the principal objectives of the original CETA legislation. Each community was to assess its manpower needs, select appropriate programs and service deliverers, and develop long-range as well as short-range plans to deal with local manpower problems. The act provided for manpower advisory councils to participate in the planning process. However, prior to EJPEA, Title II and Title VI plans were essentially fiscal documents to justify grants, with added details as to how funds were to be spent (National Research Council, 1978b, Chapter 3). And since PSE decisions were typically made by public officials, the planning council before EJPEA had little influence on public service employment decisions. EJPEA, however, required prime sponsors to clear PSE project proposals with the planning councils and prohibited the sponsor from disapproving a project proposal without considering comments of the council and providing the applicant and the planning council with a written statement of its reasons for disapproval.

Although EJPEA and the PSE expansion resulted in increased tactical planning, there was no improvement in overall strategic planning. The focus has been on preparing hiring schedules, developing PSE projects, and consulting with planning councils on the merits of project proposals. But, EJPEA has had little or no effect on the development of comprehensive planning—analyzing the characteristics and needs of the unemployed population, the community resources necessary to meet these needs, labor market conditions, and laying out responsive programs. However, it opened up more options for dealing with local problems.

Sponsors, for the most part, limited themselves to following administrative rules and requirements to qualify for PSE funds. This was due as much to a lack of emphasis on coordinated planning in the entire program as to the haste with which the PSE expansion was launched. In addition, sponsors were implementing new youth programs, which also required planning activities. The accumulation of separately funded programs for specific purposes has further compartmentalized planning.

MAJOR CONSIDERATIONS IN PSE PLANNING

The major concern of CETA administrators and planning officials has been the timely preparation of the grant application and the development of projects that could be implemented easily and rapidly. All of the CETA administrators who were interviewed rated the meeting of DOL hiring schedules as important (Table 7). Developing projects consistent with public service needs and with the abilities of participants were also significant factors but less frequently rated as important planning considerations. Only 3 of the 28 CETA administrators interviewed said that alleviating fiscal pressure of their communities was a significant objective in planning for Title VI expansion, but regional office representatives rated fiscal pressure as an important factor in 9 areas. When CETA administrators and other respondents were questioned about the effects of public service employment, their responses differed; there was more recognition that projects as well as regular public service jobs tend to ease fiscal pressures (see Chapter 7).

Members of planning councils and CETA administrators had similar perceptions of factors that were important in planning strategy, except that council members were less frequently concerned with DOL hiring pressure and more often interested in seeing that PSE projects meet local public service needs.

Other factors that figured in PSE planning were the need to balance the distribution of public service jobs among government agencies and nonprofit organizations and among local governments within the jurisdiction of the prime sponsor. While many CETA administrators in the sample were concerned with finding projects suitable for the skills of the applicant population, only one considered the training potential of PSE jobs to be an important planning consideration.

TABLE 7   Considerations of Local Officials in Planning for Public Service Employment Expansion, Sample Prime Sponsor Areas

	Order of Importance[a]	
Considerations in Planning	CETA Administrators	Planning Council Chairmen
Meeting DOL hiring schedule	1	3
Projects consistent with local public service needs	2	1
Projects consistent with skills of eligible persons	2	2
Maintenance of effort	3	4
Concern over capacity of local governments to absorb PSE workers	4	5
Alleviating fiscal pressures of local governments	5	6

[a] Ranked in descending order of frequency.

COORDINATION IN PLANNING

Coordinated planning for PSE and Title I programs would be useful for both Title I trainees, who could benefit from public service work experience, and for the many PSE enrollees who could benefit from employability development services. However, there was little evidence of such coordination. The rationale was that planning for jobs involves a different set of institutions and decision makers than planning for Title I activities and that differences among titles in eligibility, activities, and delivery agencies, as well as timing of plans and procedures for consultation with planning councils, made it difficult to combine planning for all titles.

Pressure to meet deadlines for submitting grant applications left little time for sophisticated planning. The situation was aggravated by difficulties in obtaining data to identify public service needs and to determine the number of eligible participants in each of the categories specified in the legislation. There were also problems in consolidating the employment requirements of jurisdictions and agencies seeking PSE positions. Frequent changes in signals and unreasonable demands by some federal personnel complicated planning.

While there was no formal coordination of PSE and Title I planning, there were some indirect effects. Three prime sponsors planned to drop adult work experience and public service employment from their Title I programs, since these kinds of activities could be funded under Title VI.

One sponsor planned to adjust Title I programs to lower skilled persons since opportunities for those with higher skills were available under Title VI. Another arranged to use the same instructors to teach basic life skills to both Title I and Title VI participants.

Coordinated planning was also infrequent for the PSE programs—Titles II and VI—although preparation of grants for the two programs are usually handled by the same CETA office. In Phoenix, there was even complete separation of responsibility for operation of the PSE programs. A Job Stimulus Department was set up to handle projects, while Title VI nonproject programs and Title II were handled by other government departments.

The Department of Labor has taken some steps to promote consolidated planning. Under guidelines issued in mid-1977, core elements of various grant applications have been combined into a prime sponsor agreement that does not change from year to year. Attachments and modifications for each program are to be appended annually. This concept was later adopted in the CETA reauthorization act (Public Law 95-524). While this approach reduces paperwork, it does not basically alter the underlying pattern of separate planning for each categorical grant.

LOCUS OF DECISION MAKING

EJPEA has broadened participation in PSE decisions. In addition to the planning council's review of projects, employment service agencies were involved in selecting clients, community-based organizations in questions relating to projects for nonprofit organizations, and regional office representatives with respect to hiring schedules. However, final determinations are made by CETA administrators in consultation with local elected officials.

The CETA administrator and staff were identified most frequently as the key decision makers. This influence derives from the knowledge accumulated by those intimately familiar with the complex regulations, procedures, and operations of CETA. Nonetheless, in Ramsey and Stanislaus counties, two relatively small areas, the planning councils exercised the most responsibility, and in several other areas the council shared that responsibility with the CETA administrator.

The magnitude of funds and the number of positions in the PSE expansion attracted the attention of local elected officials (or chief administrative officials), particularly in large cities, where they exercise control and provide general guidance to CETA staff. In nine areas, elected officials were identified as chief decision makers, either alone or in combination with CETA administrators. In several consortia and balance-of-state programs, decisions are made at the subsponsor level, with the participation of the elected officials. Typically, elected or administrative officials were involved in deciding on the proportion of funds to allot to nonprofit agencies and in the selection of projects.

The CETA reauthorization act provides that the planning council chairman must be selected from "public" (nongovernment) members. This does not necessarily affect the decision-making role of elected officials in PSE, nor would it be desirable to do so, given the basic premise of CETA to establish accountability at the local political level.

THE PLANNING COUNCIL

In an effort to increase community participation, EJPEA assigned a significant operating function, the review and recommendation of PSE projects, to local manpower planning councils. There was some variation in the extent of council participation in the project review. In more than one-third of the cases studied, review by the council was described as pro forma, and in most of the remaining areas the councils did not fully review proposals because of the complexity of the program, the tight schedule, and the sheer volume (see Chapter 9). Although project review generated more activity for planning councils and required more time from their members, it has not resulted in more effective participation in the basic planning process. In fact, some respondents reported that new PSE project demands on the council's time reduced their capacity to participate in the analysis of local manpower needs and in decisions as to how these needs could best be met.

Few areas in the sample reported changes in planning council membership attributable to EJPEA. Changes that did occur resulted from normal turnover and other reasons unrelated to EJPEA, such as the addition of a youth employment council. Only two areas reported an expansion of membership attributable to EJPEA. In Ramsey County, members of the personnel committee of the county board were added to review governmental project proposals. In Cook County, the planning council was expanded to include more representatives of program agents.

PLANNING IN CONSORTIA AND BALANCE OF STATES

Planning and decision making are more complex in prime sponsor areas such as counties, consortia, and balance of states, which encompass program agents or other subjurisdictions.[1] Two patterns have emerged in these situations: 9 areas—most of them small—have centralized their planning, while 13—mainly larger areas or balance of states—have decentralized planning responsibility.

About half of the prime sponsors with decentralized planning gave program agents or other subjurisdictions almost carte blanche in drawing up projects and planning PSE operations. The other half exercised some control either in the preparation or the review stage. In the Cleveland consortium, component political jurisdictions drew up lists of government projects for review at consortium level by CETA administrative staff and ratification by the consortium executive board and the advisory council. However, decisions for private nonprofit agency projects went directly to the consortium staff and the advisory council.

For the most part there were only minor problems in reconciling plans of subjurisdictions. The Orange County consortium, with a particularly complex structure, reported problems in meshing hiring and expenditure schedules. Other areas reported delays in getting materials and documentation due to the layering of planning units.

The balance-of-state areas, because of their unwieldy size, completely decentralized planning for PSE expansion. In Maine, each county makes its own decisions in consultation with its planning council; the state prime sponsor merely reviews and consolidates local plans. In Arizona, four councils of government (COGs), each representing a combination of counties, have the key planning responsibility within a framework set at the state level. When plans are submitted, approval by the CETA administrator and the balance-of-state council is pro forma. North Carolina, while centralizing administration of PSE programs at the state level, delegates planning to counties. In the Balance of Texas, plans for 131 counties are consolidated at 15 substate planning units and are reviewed at the prime sponsor level only for conformance with regulations.

EFFECT ON ORGANIZATION AND MANAGEMENT

EJPEA and the PSE expansion, in addition to generating heavier workloads, affected local administration in three major ways: (1) They necessitated a more complex method of control and accountability to deal with the increased number of subcontractors; (2) the requirements for rapid certification of participant eligibility encouraged closer relationships with

---

[1]Program agents are cities or counties of 50,000 or more located within the jurisdiction of a prime sponsor. The act gives program agents responsibility for administering public service employment programs consistent with the prime sponsor's overall grant application.

the employment service; and (3) the expansion and increased funding for PSE increased awareness of the public officials of the potentialities of CETA for filling public service needs, resulting in a more politically visible program.

In the process, CETA became identified more as a method of arranging for public service jobs and less as a means of training and job development for the hard-core unemployed, although most of the CETA staff and the members of advisory committees interviewed for this study acknowledge that Title I programs may be more responsive to the manpower needs of the community. They provide a wider range of services and have a better tie-in to the private sector, where most employment opportunities are found. However, some respondents noted the advantages of public service employment as a more direct means of giving clients work experience and income.

ORGANIZATIONAL STRUCTURE

Before EJPEA, local CETA organizations ranged from small multifunctional staffs in some areas to highly compartmentalized bureaucracies. The size of staff and scope of activities depended not only on the size of the jurisdiction but also on the extent to which manpower services were contracted out or handled directly by the CETA administrator. Nearly everywhere, all PSE programs were handled by the same office.

Prime sponsors surveyed did not find it necessary to undertake major reorganizations despite the heavier workload. The PSE expansion was accomplished largely within the framework of the existing organizational structure in all but two of the study areas: As previously stated, one of these, Phoenix, established a new job stimulus department to administer PSE project functions. The other, St. Paul, departed from its tightly integrated delivery system to establish a transitional employment unit for PSE. This separated the responsibility for PSE from Title I programs.

The most immediate effect of the PSE expansion was an increase in administrative staff. An analysis of expenditures suggests that CETA state and local administrative positions rose from 20,000 man-year equivalents in 1976 to 33,000 by fiscal 1978.[2] This includes administrative positions of

[2]Estimates based on administrative expenditures for Titles I, II, and VI using an assumed cost per man-year based on employment service experience. Administrative expenditures are costs associated with management and related costs for materials and supplies. EJPEA increased allowable administrative expenditures from 10 percent to 15 percent of Title VI allotments. The estimated administrative positions do not include instructors, counselors, or other personnel who provide manpower services either for the prime sponsors, schools, or other subcontractors. If the full-time equivalents for these program operations were added, the estimate would be more than double the 33,000 administrative positions.

TABLE 8 Total and Administrative Expenditures, CETA Titles II and VI, Fiscal 1976-1978 (millions of dollars)

Title	Total Expenditures			Administrative Expenditures			Administrative Expenditures as a Percent of Total		
	Fiscal 1976[a]	Fiscal 1977	Fiscal 1978	Fiscal 1976[a]	Fiscal 1977	Fiscal 1978	Fiscal 1976[a]	Fiscal 1977	Fiscal 1978
TOTAL	2,517.0	2,585.7	5,756.1	93.4	152.2	414.9	3.7	5.9	7.2
II	561.4	864.0	1,022.2	26.0	50.5	67.7	4.6	5.9	6.5
VI	1,955.6	1,721.7	4,733.9	67.4	101.7	347.2	3.5	5.9	7.3

SOURCE: Employment and Training Administration, U.S. Department of Labor.

[a] July 1975-June 1976.

subcontractors as well as prime sponsors, but does not include CETA positions assigned to the state employment service and unemployment insurance agencies. These also rose sharply, from 6,700 in 1976 to 9,300 in 1978.

The staff increases were reflected in administrative costs for PSE. Administrative expenditures for Titles II and VI increased from $93 to $152 million between 1976 and 1977 and to $415 in fiscal 1978 as prime sponsors geared up for the expansion (Table 8). More important, the ratio of administrative to total costs nearly doubled, from 3.7 percent in fiscal 1976 to 7.2 percent in 1978, but still remained far below the authorized level of 15 percent for Title VI under EJPEA. In 22 of the 28 prime sponsor areas in the study, costs climbed more than 20 percent between 1976 and 1977. In more than two-thirds of the 28 cases, the ratio of administrative to total outlays also went up between the 2 years, indicating higher administrative costs for EJPEA than for the regular PSE programs. Problems in managing within cost limits are discussed further below.

MANAGEMENT PROBLEMS

Most sponsors ran into new and difficult administrative problems in setting up pools of eligible applicants, arranging to determine and verify eligibility, identifying prospective employing agencies, soliciting and reviewing project proposals, and negotiating and supervising contracts. These responsibilities complicated budgeting, reporting, and financial accounting. Sponsors had to deal with large numbers of PSE subcontractors over whom they had less direct control than in other CETA programs. The size of the expansion and the urgent hiring schedule generated a crisis atmosphere in some prime sponsor agencies that added to the management problems.

The sponsors studied considered the time required to handle PSE projects—about 5 or 10 times as much as the time required for regular PSE, according to one estimate—to be excessive in terms of the needs of other programs. In about half of the areas, the preoccupation of staff with PSE project operations during the buildup phase reduced their ability to administer other titles, particularly Title I. Most of the sample sponsors faced problems resulting from changes in regulations; numerous field directives, as well as the sheer volume of paperwork; and the time constraints.

Staffing, contract supervision, merit systems, and handling retirement funds were the most prevalent areas of difficulty. Half the sponsors in the sample reported that staff and space requirements were a major problem. In Cleveland, for example, the PSE coordinator administered the entire PSE operation at the consortium level almost single-handed until five PSE participants were taken on to help him. The professional staff in Chester County grew from 2 full-time and 17 part-time employees for all CETA titles to 24 full-time staff members. Even where staff was added, there were problems in training and supervising people unfamiliar with CETA.

Problems of supervision of contracts, verification of eligibility, monitoring, or obtaining timely statistical reports were reported in the areas surveyed. Neither government nor nonprofit operators of projects were familiar with CETA, and both groups needed supervision. However, the monitoring system was described in some instances as cursory—merely checking to see if participants were on the job. Verification of eligibility was usually left to the employment service, and often determinations were based on self-certification by applicants; client data were not checked adequately (see Chapter 5). Sponsors relied on data from subcontractors as a means of monitoring; but this data was frequently unreliable, and some sponsors reported delays in obtaining reports.

Merit systems complicated the enrollment of PSE employees in 8 of 28 sample areas. Requirements varied; in Kansas City and Topeka, CETA applicants were required to take merit service tests only for positions in police and fire departments, while in Phoenix participants had to pass civil service tests for any position. In Chester County and Orange County, some subjurisdictions required entrance tests, while others did not. In New York and Philadelphia, however, CETA workers were hired outside the civil service system. While this avoided the immediate problem of delay in taking on CETA workers, it was a handicap to their ultimate absorption in regular civil service posts. This illustrates a typical kind of trade-off: the objective of quickly enrolling disadvantaged persons into PSE jobs versus the ultimate goal of moving some of these individuals into the regular civil service.

There were no provisions for blanketing CETA workers into regular jobs in areas with highly structured merit systems; transition from CETA to regular jobs required passing a competitive examination. In New York, the union favors classifying CETA employees as competitive rather than provisional workers. This would give them an advantage in taking examinations since their on-the-job experience would be credited.

In most areas studied there were few union issues involving PSE employment. In four areas—including New York and Philadelphia—CETA workers were required to belong to employee unions under a union shop arrangement. Unions in Orange County were involved in negotiating job titles, and in New York the unions prevented the city from hiring CETA employees for positions comparable to those of laid-off regular workers.

Retirement fund payments posed a dilemma for most sponsors. A new Department of Labor regulation forbidding sponsors to make payments to retirement systems on behalf of CETA employees unless those employees receive credit toward their own retirement was very controversial. The department's ruling was based on the rationale that CETA funds are intended for wages and salaries. Although the act requires CETA employees to receive the same fringe benefits as others similarly employed, it was not intended that CETA funds be drained off into retirement systems in which CETA workers would not be eligible to participate. The department's regulation did permit retirement contributions to be held in a special account to cover costs for CETA workers who acquire permanent status or who transfer to employment where their retirement credits can be used. In some states, notably California, the retirement system does not permit CETA participants already enrolled in state systems to withdraw from the system. Since DOL would not permit use of CETA funds, sponsors, in some cases, were obliged to use funds from local tax sources for contributions to the retirement fund on behalf of CETA employees.[3]

Some nonprofit organizations sponsoring PSE projects reported cash flow difficulties. The problem is particularly acute where the subcontractor pays wages and is reimbursed by the CETA administrator. Nonprofit organizations said that they were not in a position to advance funds from their own resources pending reimbursement.

Sponsors interviewed at the time of the survey had not yet faced the need for job development and placement. Since projects for the most part had a number of months to run, the question of how to terminate them and how to find suitable unsubsidized jobs for participants was deferred. The immediate priorities were to fill available positions, meet hiring schedules, and get workers on the payroll as quickly as possible.

PROGRAM AGENT AND BALANCE-OF-STATE ADMINISTRATION

Counties, consortia, and balance-of-state areas that have program agent cities or counties within their jurisdictions have more complicated administrative processes than those programs which operate within a

---

[3]Under the CETA reauthorization act, no CETA funds may be used for contributions to retirement funds for participants enrolled after July 1, 1979, unless the contribution bears a reasonable relationship to the cost of providing benefits to participants.

single jurisdiction. Communication and accounting are obviously affected by the layers of administration, but the more basic problem is obtaining agreement between the prime sponsor's objective and those of the subjurisdictions.

Where there were program agents, administration as well as planning for public service employment was usually decentralized to their level, but the degree of autonomy varied. In three cases, program agents relied completely on the prime sponsor; in other areas, prime sponsors exercised some control, either through formal review of program agent plans or through informal relationships. The Lansing consortium affords a good example of a highly structured relationship between the prime sponsor and program agents. There, each program agent issues requests for proposals (RFPs). Projects are reviewed by the program agent board, consisting of three councilmen, who assign priorities based on per capita costs, skill level, and ratio of administration to total cost. Projects are then sent to the consortium staff and to the manpower planning council, which make recommendations to the consortium administrative board. When a project is approved, the program agent assumes responsibility for its administration. This process of clearing each proposal through both the program agent and prime sponsor levels becomes enormously complex, and the potential for conflicts is compounded.

Other problems reported by program agents are similar to those of prime sponsors. They include lack of lead time for developing projects, reluctance to involve nonprofit organizations, delays in obtaining applicant referral from the employment service, reluctance on the part of government agencies to undertake commitments to hire PSE employees because of uncertainty of continued funding, and difficulty in obtaining reports from community-based organizations.

Balance-of-state sponsors also tend to decentralize responsibilities to their subjurisdictions. The expansion of public service employment did not create new problems, but tended to place additional strains on staff resources and on an administrative system designed for smaller systems and lower levels of funding. The breakup of three balance-of-state areas into smaller units for convenience in administration reflected fundamental problems inherent in vast distances and disparate economic conditions.

ADMINISTRATIVE FUNDS

Under EJPEA, 85 percent of the funds allocated to prime sponsors for Title VI was to be used for participant wages and fringe benefits, leaving 15 percent for all other costs such as rent, supplies, equipment, the hiring of non-CETA employees for management or supervisory positions, training of participants, and other administrative costs. The previously authorized amount was 10 percent.

In 15 of the 28 areas, the prime sponsor permitted project operators to use the full 15 percent authorized for nonwage costs, but in 13 areas they restricted project operators to a lesser percentage. In 3 of these areas, project operators were not allowed any CETA funds for administration and were forced to defray these costs with their own funds or by using project enrollees for supervisory or other administrative tasks. In 10 areas, project operators were allowed between 7.5 and 14 percent. When prime sponsors set ceilings under 15 percent, they used some or all of the difference for their own administrative costs.

Keeping overhead below authorized levels was supposed to free funds to hire more unemployed persons, but in a few instances the tight fist may in fact have impeded hiring. Among the few sponsors in the sample who fell short of their Title VI hiring schedule was one that allowed no nonwage costs to project operators and another that did not provide for rent or materials and restricted amounts for other administrative purposes.

In 19 of the 28 study areas, local officials believed that the 15 percent limit on the share of CETA funds that could be used for administration had affected project design or operation. In most of these areas, the limitation resulted in a greater emphasis on labor-intensive projects rather than on projects that sponsors would have preferred but that entailed higher materials or supervisory costs. In that sense, the limitation helped to achieve the major objective of CETA PSE—to maximize job opportunities.

In 4 of the 19 areas, local officials said that the limited funds for nonwage purposes precluded training and employablity development services for project participants. However, the absence of those services appeared to be due more to the pressure for speedy implementation and the perception of Title VI as a job creation rather than to an employability development program. A few areas attributed poor record keeping or supervision to inadequate funds for administration.[4]

Generally, nonprofit organizations were more likely to be affected by limited administrative funds than government agencies. This was a function of size. Smaller organizations generally did not have the space, equipment, or supervisors to be spared or shared for project administration, and this discouraged some from proposing projects.

The minimum share of PSE funds that must be spent on participant wages and benefits was reduced from 85 percent to 80 percent in the 1978

---

[4]Although sponsors reported that they are hampered by lack of administrative funds, they apparently use less than they are entitled to. The $152.2 million spent for Titles II and VI in 1977 amounts to 5.9 percent of total expenditures—far below the 15 percent authorized by the act for salaries, rent, equipment, and other overhead (see Table 8).

reauthorization of CETA. The new act also earmarked funds for training and employability services in Title VI—10 percent of total for fiscal year 1979 and 5 percent thereafter. The remaining funds—10 percent in 1979 and 15 percent thereafter—are available for administration and other costs. The reduction in the funds available for administration and supplies from 15 percent to 10 percent of total in 1979 is less likely to inhibit government-operated programs than projects operated by nonprofit agencies.[5]

COORDINATING WITH OTHER PROGRAMS

Better coordination and linking of employment, training, and related programs have long been sought and were among the justifications for CETA.[6] It was assumed that local and state officials who are responsible for related federal and local programs would coordinate them with CETA, but the potential has never been fully realized. When EJPEA came along there was again expectation for increased cooperation; but results have been mixed, with little progress in providing ancillary services to CETA employees, but some new joint activities.

PSE AND OTHER CETA PROGRAMS

Sponsors, with few exceptions, manage PSE programs separately from Title I CETA programs, and staff, procedures, and clients tend to be different. There appears to be little effort to harmonize the various CETA programs, although local officials agree that such linkage would enrich public service employment by offering participants a wider range of services. Coordination of the employability development programs of Title I with the PSE programs of Title VI would be advantageous for participants of both programs.

Although 24 of the 28 sponsors in the study believed that tightening of the PSE eligibility criteria and thus reaching a less skilled population would increase the need for employability development services, most made no

---

[5]The CETA reauthorization act permits the comingling of adminstrative funds under various titles.

[6]For purposes of this discussion a distinction is made between "linkage" and "coordination." "Linkage" refers to a cooperative arrangement to provide ancillary services or training to CETA PSE enrollees not usually available to them as part of a regular PSE program. Day-care services provided to PSE participants by a local public or private social service agency would be an example. "Coordination" refers to (a) arrangements among various programs or agencies with similar objectives or (b) cooperation among agencies with different goals to promote the objectives of each.

attempt to use the Title I funds for such services. The needs of new PSE participants most often cited by sponsors were for transportation, day care, skill training, remedial education, and training in job search techniques. Sponsors who saw no need for employability development services stated that participants selected were generally the better qualified job-ready individuals.

Almost all sponsors cited lack of funds and time as reasons for not providing new PSE participants the support and training they believed were necessary. Funds for employability development may come from two sources: the 15 percent of PSE dollars allotted for administration and Title VI program funds. In fiscal 1977, only 5.9 percent of PSE expenditures went for administration and in fiscal 1978, only 7.2 percent. With respect to Title VI program funds, DOL reports show that less than 0.2 percent was spent on both classroom and on-the-job training in 1977. While 8 of the 28 sponsors in the study used Title I funds to provide employability development services for PSE participants, the amounts, with two exceptions, were negligible.

Since sponsors were not fully using their Title VI administrative funds or diverting funds from Title I, it does not appear that the absence of supportive programs for Title VI participants can be attributed to the lack of funds. The reason most often cited for the lack of program coordination was that the speed of the PSE buildup did not permit time for it. However, as ETA officials point out, sponsors were informed of the need for expansion more than 3 months before the start-up date of the expansion.

The more likely reasons for the limited number of supportive programs available to the new PSE participants are the administrative difficulties in tying programs together. The structure and funding of CETA programs do not facilitate ties among its various titles or with other federally funded programs. The separate reporting and accounting required for each CETA title generates an administrative burden. It is difficult to accurately prorate costs and activities when programs are jointly funded or serve the same participants. As one field observer noted, sponsors "perceive the programs (Title I and PSE) as serving different people with different needs, requiring discrete networks." For the most part, sponsor management of the PSE program parallels the practices used to hire, assign, and manage regular employees. Thus, PSE participants are treated the same as regular employees and usually receive only those services that were available to regular employees.

For the most part, sponsors did not attempt to coordinate public service employment programs with the Title III programs for Indians, migrant and seasonal farm workers, and other disadvantaged groups. However, 8 of the 28 sponsors reported that PSE project participants were assigned to Title III projects, which are administered directly by the national office of the Department of Labor. Several used PSE participants as instructors, supervisors, or monitors for youth programs. In Chester County, for example, Title VI slots were allotted to a farm worker project to assist in locating jobs, housing, schools, and health services for migrants who would not otherwise be helped. In the Balance of Arizona, local operators of Title III migrant and Indian programs were informed of opportunities in PSE programs. In the Balance of Texas, however, 20 percent of all Title I, II, and VI CETA funds are earmarked by the governor for migrant programs administered through the local councils of government without any contact with Title III migrant programs administered by nonprofit organizations in the same areas.

The basic reasons for lack of coordination with Title III programs are the same as those discussed earlier: separate grants, eligibility rules, reporting and accounting systems, and the difficulty in maintaining control and accountability. According to one observer, " . . . the PSE staff are basically insular in their concerns and desire to avoid the external evaluation which is concomitant with cooperative exercises."

TIES WITH OTHER FEDERAL PROGRAMS AND WITH LOCAL
INSTITUTIONS

Although there was little linkage with other programs to provide services to PSE participants, other forms of coordination do exist. About half of the 28 respondents in the sample reported working with other federally funded programs (in addition to the ES and WIN programs where cooperation is mandated). Ten sponsors were cooperating in federally funded home improvement or weatherization projects for low-income families. In Phoenix, for example, the Urban League sponsored a housing rehabilitation project using the city's community development allotment for materials and supplies and ETA for subsidized labor.

Rigidities in the rules of government programs discourage coordination with economic development projects. Typically a local government with economic development funds solicits bids from private contractors, who are not permitted to use CETA PSE employees. However, cooperation can be arranged with private employers through on-the-job training or hiring terminees from CETA programs.

In virtually all areas in the sample, prime sponsors are providing CETA PSE participants to community-based organizations and other nonprofit agencies.[7] This gives CETA considerable leverage that could be used to promote developmental programs for CETA enrollees or to obtain needed support services. However, the potential for coordination is not being realized; there were few cases where reciprocal arrangements were in effect. One of these was Union County, where housing projects, senior citizen projects, and day-care centers all had PSE participants. In an exchange arrangement, a day-care center agreed to reserve 40 percent of its openings to accommodate CETA enrollees. The Calhoun County prime sponsor entered into a nonfinancial agreement with the Department of Social Services and the Department of Health to supply services for CETA clients without cost to CETA. In rural Maine, where resources are few, community-based organizations were able to provide some training and supportive services to PSE participants assigned to them.

EMPLOYMENT SERVICE ROLE IN PSE EXPANSION

CETA established a new national employment and training system alongside of the existing employment service network without clarifying the relationship between them. The employment service was no longer the presumptive deliverer of manpower services and was toppled from its place as the primary manpower agency. In many areas, activities such as placement and OJT were either taken over by sponsors or subcontracted to other organizations in the community. Although a follow-up study made during the second year of CETA showed some recovery of activities in Titles II and VI, particularly in balance-of-state areas, on the whole relationships that developed between the two groups were strained (National Research Council, 1978b, pp. 149–55). Field observers examining these relationships late in 1977 and early in 1978, after the passage of EJPEA and the PSE expansion, reported less rivalry and increased cooperation overall. However, this broad conclusion obscures many local variations and nuances.

The Employment and Training Administration assigned a significant role to the employment service in the PSE expansion. It centered around PSE intake activities (interviewing UI claimants and WIN participants to determine their availability for the new PSE jobs, developing a pool of PSE eligibles, and verifying the eligibility of applicants) and was designed to achieve a number of objectives in addition to enhancing the role of the

[7]"Community-based organizations," as used in this report, means organizations that normally represent or serve specific groups in a community. They include such organizations as the Urban League, Opportunities Industrialization Centers, community action agencies, and community development organizations.

employment service. ETA hoped that having the employment service develop a pool of eligible applicants that the sponsors could immediately hire for the new PSE jobs would speed the PSE expansion. The use of the employment service was also expected to facilitate the hiring of UI claimants and AFDC recipients, two target groups with which the employment service had close contact; and, finally, employment service handling of PSE intake would, it was believed, reduce duplication.

To ensure employment service participation, ETA requested sponsors to enter into formal agreements with local ES offices, which spelled out responsibilities for recruitment, referral, and eligibility verification of PSE participants. The regional office performance in arranging for these agreements was monitored by the ETA national office, and consequently the pressure that regional staff put upon sponsors was quite intense. One sponsor understood that the new PSE funds would not be granted until the sponsor had completed the "necessary" agreement with the local ES office.

As an inducement to prime sponsors to enter into such agreements, the federal regulations exempted sponsors from liability for mispayments to ineligible participants if the employment service, under a formal agreement with the sponsor, had verified the eligibility of the participant. It was an offer the sponsor could not afford to turn down, and when added to the urgings of the regional office, it is not surprising that 26 of the 28 sponsors in the study signed such agreements. Of these, 24 were cooperative, nonfinancial agreements and the remaining 2 contracts were in areas where the relationship between the sponsor and the employment service was particularly strained.

In 9 of the 26 areas, the PSE agreements were addenda to umbrella agreements covering other CETA activities, while in the other 17 areas the agreements were restricted to the PSE expansion. But even in these 17 areas, sponsors had other limited agreements or contracts with the employment service covering specific functions or programs. Indeed, formal agreements are not new to the CETA/ES relationship; most of the 28 sponsors studied had some kind of agreement with the employment service prior to the PSE expansion. The difference was that the PSE agreements were literally mandated by ETA, while the others were voluntary.

The cooperative agreements covered a wide range. Most often they included activities essential to the expansion: eligibility verification, applicant screening and interviewing, notification of potential eligibles, special listing of PSE job openings with the employment service for referral of veterans, file search, operation of the PSE pool, coordination with other recruitment efforts, and referral of applicants to hiring agencies. Further, the agreements did not necessarily include all the activities which local ES offices provided to sponsors. Seven of the formal agreements, for example,

TABLE 9   Activities Provided by the Employment Service for Public
Service Employment Expansion, Sample Prime Sponsor Areas

Activities	Percent of Sponsors with Agreements	
	Included in CETA/ES Agreement	Provided by ES Without Agreement
Eligibility verification	92	4
Applicant screening and interviewing	88	8
Special listing of PSE job openings for veterans	85	19
Notifications of potential eligibles	81	19
File search	69	23
Coordination with other recruitment efforts	65	27
Operation of PSE pool	65	12
Referral of applicants to hiring agencies	62	12
Outreach	50	19
Publicizing availability of PSE jobs	50	23
Direct placement	42	23
Labor market information	27	58
Selection of participants	27	0
Indirect placement	27	19
Testing	15	35
Counseling	8	38
Title VI project development	4	12
Number of Sponsors with ES Agreements	(26)	—

included labor market information although this service was provided to
sponsors in at least 15 other areas without a formal agreement (see Table
9).

While ES services covered by the nonfinancial agreements were provided
at no cost, all but one of the local offices in the 28 sponsor areas studied
reported work load increases as a result of the PSE expansion. In three
areas the increase was negligible, but in the remainder it was significant.
The resource issue, often a stumbling block to agreement in the past, was
resolved by the "coin" of the program—dollars and PSE slots. Employment service offices received placement credit for referrals hired in PSE
openings, which in turn increased their relative allotments from ES federal
grant funds. Moreover, 16 of the sponsors made positions available to the
ES offices to offset increased work load, a gesture that made negotiations
less contentious and agreements easier to formulate.

CETA PSE placements are becoming a very sizable proportion of all ES

TABLE 10 Individuals Placed by the Employment Service, by Class of Placement, Fiscal 1976-1978 (thousands)

Fiscal Year	Total Individuals Placed by ES	Placed in CETA			Placed in WIN	
		On-the-Job Training	Public Service Employment	Work Experience	On-the-Job Training	Public Service Employment
Number of Individuals						
1976	3,367	38	201	149	20	10
1977	4,138	54	334	384	27	10
1978	4,623	63	579	466	29	8
Percent of Total						
1976	100	1	6	4	1	a
1977	100	1	8	9	1	a
1978	100	1	13	10	1	a

SOURCE: Employment and Training Administration, U.S. Department of Labor.

a Less than 0.5 percent.

placements as result of ES participation in the PSE expansion. In fiscal 1977, 8 percent of all individuals placed by employment service offices were in CETA public service employment openings. By 1978 the proportion rose to 12.5 percent. Combined with individuals placed in summer programs for youth and in Title I programs, CETA accounts for about one-fourth of all individuals placed by the employment service (Table 10). In 1978, individuals placed by the employment service in CETA PSE positions accounted for nearly 90 percent of all the 646,000 new enrollees in Title II and Title VI CETA programs. This reflects the fact that employment service offices received placement credit for individuals recruited by sponsors who were then sent to the employment service office for pro forma eligibility checks.

Another policy that affected ES/CETA relationships was the cooperative development of pools of PSE eligibles to provide a ready supply of persons necessary for a rapid expansion of the program. Enrollment focused, particularly on eligible UI claimants and AFDC recipients, two of the four target groups identified by Congress in the EJPEA. Sixteen sponsors relied entirely on employment service pools; eight maintained separate PSE pools (three of these sponsors also using the ES pool). Four sponsors did not use any pool (see Chapter 5).

Analysis of the PSE expansion suggests that some of the objectives that ETA had hoped to achieve by designating a PSE role for the employment service were not fully realized. For one, there was no difference in the proportion of AFDC recipients and UI claimants hired by sponsors who relied heavily upon ES for intake activities and those who did not.

While use of the employment service was increased in PSE intake activities prior to the expansion, this trend was significantly hastened thereby. But the employment service role in Title I has remained unchanged. The fractiousness so evident earlier has subsided, and rough edges have been smoothed by ES and CETA staffs working together to meet tight deadlines and achieve common goals. But many joint efforts were undertaken only at the insistance of the Employment and Training Administration, and some may be abandoned as soon as it is deemed propitious. Such was the fate of the ES pools. At least one sponsor allowed the ES/CETA agreement to lapse at the end of its 6-month term.

The survey found no evidence that PSE expansion or ETA policies have appreciably reduced the duplication of activities of the two institutions. Moreover, ETA policy on the use of ES to verify participant eligibility has in some instances resulted in both the PSE and the ES performing this function.

To summarize the nature of the current relationship, sponsors were categorized on the basis of whether CETA/ES relationships were predominantly negative or positive. In 22 the relationship was judged to be positive. The remaining 6 were equally divided between those where the relationship was clearly negative and those where it was mixed.

One indication of improving relationships is that few major problems cropped up during the last year. Eight of the 28 areas reported some difficulties. ES officials complained about sponsors' restrictive or vague job specifications, while sponsors criticized the employment service for too few referrals, failure to reach specific groups or geographic areas, or processing delays.

On the whole, there is greater agreement on the ES role in CETA. There has been a shift away from the extremes of complete exclusion or of a presumptive role for the employment service in all employment and training programs. The developing consensus is that the employment service does have an important but limited role in CETA, focusing on intake for PSE programs and the referral of persons with structural handicaps to Title I programs. ES officials embraced this definition of their role more enthusiastically than sponsors, particularly with respect to PSE intake functions. Of the 28 sponsors studied, 3 resented being "coerced" by ETA to use the employment service in the expansion; 4 mistrusted the employment service (they felt that it was using PSE activities to enhance its placement record); 3 others expressed dissatisfaction, not so much with the role as with its performance.

Improvement of CETA/ES relationships stems from several additional factors. The CETA staff, now with several years of experience and confident of its position, appears less fearful of a local rival. In a number of areas, changes in leadership improved relationships. New personnel appeared to have placed better relationships high on their agendas and achieved them. The joint experience of both organizations in implementing the PSE expansion has also helped.

RECENTRALIZATION

The original CETA legislation placed control over local manpower programs with state and local officials. It also mandated federal oversight responsibility but left vague the boundaries of federal and local authority. However, each amendment to CETA has projected the Department of Labor more actively into the local scene. This trend toward recentralization was accentuated by EJPEA and the rapid expansion of PSE. The CETA reauthorization act of 1978 continued this course.

While federal–local relationships vary, 16 of the 28 sponsors surveyed reported increased supervision by regional office staff. Regional offices kept close tabs on the local hiring buildup. Beyond that, their influence was felt through such measures as interpreting new regulations, insistence upon the use of the employment service in the PSE expansion, and restricting payments into the local retirement system. In a few areas the regional office role declined because problems requiring their attention had been resolved. Turnover of federal representatives continued to be a serious problem; one area saw three federal representatives in 1 year, and the third was about to be replaced at the time of the survey.

Relations between local sponsors and state governments were not significantly affected, since the states have virtually no role in managing local PSE programs except in the balance of states. The only connection between local PSE programs and state governments was the use of state agencies or institutions as employment sites for local PSE positions. However, in 13 of the survey areas few positions were allotted to state agencies. Even in state capitals, where opportunities for such employment abound, there were problems in assigning PSE workers to state jobs: Civil service requirements impeded hirings, the required skills were not available among applicants, and difficulties were anticipated in supervising temporary employees. In 10 local areas that did place workers in state agencies, the most frequent beneficiary was the state employment service, where additional staff was used to process PSE applicants.

SUMMARY

The revision and enlargement of the public service employment program required considerable preparation. The attention of prime sponsors was riveted on meeting the PSE expansion goals, and little was done to develop a comprehensive manpower plan that would embrace and integrate all CETA programs under a sponsor's control.

The program requirements of the new Title VI program made it more difficult to coordinate PSE and Title I planning, contrary to the expectation that CETA would facilitate comprehensive planning of the manpower needs and resources of the community.

Although the opportunity to contribute to planning by governmental and nongovernmental agencies is broadened, primary decision making still rests with CETA administrators and staff. However, the size of the PSE expansion and its growing importance in providing community services has increased the participation of elected officials in the decision-making process. Decision making in large counties, consortia, and balance of states is generally decentralized to program agents and to other subunits; varying degrees of control are exercised by prime sponsors. The effect has been to further fragment the planning process.

While Congress enlarged the role of planning councils in the review and processing of PSE projects, there has been little change in their influence, the structure of the planning councils, or in their part in overall planning.

EJPEA and the expansion of PSE imposed demands on sponsors to recruit staff, phase in new programs, and expand monitoring and supervision of PSE contracts. Despite the added workload and a succession of crises, prime sponsors were able to meet the administrative requirements made necessary by EJPEA and the PSE expansion. Existing organizational structures were adapted, with some increase in the size of staff, to the expanded work load.

The administrative procedures for PSE expansion were more complex than for Title VI sustainment and Title II programs. They involved requests for and review of project proposals, determination of applicant eligibility, contracting with governmental and nongovernmental agencies, reporting, and accounting. The inclusion of nonprofit organizations expanded the task of supervising contract performance. Concentration on Title VI diverted staff and attention from Title I, which is still perceived by local manpower officials to be the most effective CETA program for dealing with structural problems of the unemployed.

Counties, consortia, and balance of states with constituent program agents and other subjurisdictions have greater problems of communication and supervision of performance. The process of clearing project proposals with advisory councils and elected officials in subjurisdictions, as well as at the prime sponsor level, is overly complex.

The growth of CETA into a series of separate titles and programs has not been conducive to a comprehensive approach in delivery of services. Relatively few linkages were developed among CETA titles or with other local institutions for development of PSE enrollees. Sponsors did not use the leverage inherent in the PSE jobs and dollars to generate ties with other related programs in the community that would enhance the employability of the new PSE participants, even though they acknowledged the need for training and supported services.

The role of the employment service agencies in manpower activities entered a new phase under EJPEA after a period of decline. ETA policies and regulations increased the recruitment role of the employment service in the expansion of PSE programs. Its increased participation, however, did not result in better participation of the target groups than achieved in areas where it was not used, nor is there evidence of an appreciable reduction in the duplication between the two institutions. On the whole, however, the experience under EJPEA and the PSE expansion has brought the ES and CETA systems into a closer relationship.

Although CETA was vague in drawing the line between federal oversight and local responsibility, the intent was to shift the responsibility for managing manpower programs from federal to local officials. However, the effect of EJPEA, as well as other new special purpose programs, has been to increase the degree of intervention by DOL regional office staff. Sponsors were subjected to particularly heavy regional office pressure in the drive to meet hiring schedules.

5 Finding and Hiring Participants

CETA Title VI eligibility requirements were revised by the Emergency Jobs Programs Extension Act (EJPEA) to help those near the end of the unemployment line rather than those at the front. Later, these revisions were, in large part, incorporated in the CETA reauthorization act. Yet, it is the many seemingly routine decisions that make up local hiring processes that in the end determine who gets a PSE job. How job information is circulated, how applicants are guided through a screening process, who is matched against what job and referred to the selecting supervisor, and, finally, how hiring officials choose among applicants are as important to who gets hired as are the legislative criteria.

The size and timing of the PSE expansion, along with the new eligibility criteria, placed new burdens on the identification, screening, and selection processes. With many more jobs to be filled rapidly and narrowed groups of eligibles, the search for applicants had to be widened, the job–person match became more difficult, and verification of applicant eligibility became more complicated. This chapter examines the ways in which sponsors adapted to these demands and assesses the effect of sponsor recruitment and selection processes on who was hired and who failed to get hired.

With the Emergency Jobs Program Extension Act of 1976, Congress, for the first time since the depression of the 1930s required an income test of applicants for public employment. To be eligible for new Title VI jobs, applicants now had to come from low-income families— those having an income less than 70 percent of the Bureau of Labor Statistics lower income standard.[1] Congress also lengthened the required spell of unemployment from 30 days (15 days for areas of substantial unemployment) to 15 weeks. These requirements applied to all new Title VI jobs and to replacements for half of the Title VI jobs authorized as of June 1976 (generally referred to as the sustainment level). Through these changes Congress attempted to direct the PSE program more specifically to the people most in need among the unemployed.

In revising the PSE eligibility criteria, Congress identified four categories of individuals and directed that each sponsor ensure that funds be equitably allocated to jobs for these groups "in light of the composition of unemployed eligible persons served by the prime sponsor." The categories include persons who (a) have been receiving unemployment compensation for 15 weeks or more, (b) have been unemployed for 15 weeks or more but are not eligible for unemployment compensation, (c) have exhausted unemployment compensation benefits, or (d) are members of families receiving Aid to Families With Dependent Children.

FEDERAL REGULATIONS AND POLICIES

Federal regulations, which are as important as legislative language at the local level, define legislative requirements, prescribe program procedures, and assign specific roles and tasks to federal, state, and local institutions and agencies. Federal managers, in the exercise of their oversight responsibilities, also influence local programs through interpretation of rules. A review of how sponsors reacted to legislative changes must consider these factors.

Employment and Training Administration regulations and policies on finding and hiring PSE participants had two overriding objectives: to facilitate a rapid expansion of the PSE program and to reduce duplication between sponsor and employment service activities by enlarging the recruitment role of the employment service. These objectives are reflected in four ETA policies adopted for the PSE expansion and in a fifth that predated the expansion but gained new importance with it:

1. *The establishment of detailed hiring schedules to complete the* PSE *expansion in 9 months.* ETA set the general pace of the expansion and required each sponsor to establish goals within the national design (National Research Council, 1978d, pp. 20–21).

[1] The lower living standard budget when EJPEA was passed in 1976 was $9,588 for a family of four. Seventy percent of that figure was $6,712. This is higher than the more familiar Office of Management and Budget poverty level, which in 1976 was $5,815.

2. *The exemption of sponsors from liability for payments made to ineligible participants if the determination of eligibility was made by the employment service.* This policy both speeded hiring and provided an incentive to use the employment service that few sponsors refused.

3. *Directives to the employment service and the sponsors to collaborate in the formation and use of an* ES *pool of persons eligible to participate in Title VI projects.* The employment service pool was designed to ensure an immediate source of eligible persons and to provide sponsors with access to AFDC recipients and UI claimants, two target categories identified by Congress. It had the concomitant effect of enlarging the role of the employment service in the PSE recruitment process.

4. *Pressure of* ETA *staff on the sponsor to include the employment service in its recruitment process and to enter a formal agreement with the employment service.* This pressure varied not only from region to region but also among federal representatives within a region. Most sponsors accepted the policy as reasonable; in view of the size and timing of the expansion, they were glad to get whatever help they could.

5. *According full credit to the employment service for placing applicants in subsidized jobs.* Placement of job seekers has always been a central function of the employment service and is the major factor used by ETA to evaluate the performance and determine the relative allocation of funds among ES agencies. In addition, the PSE expansion provided a lot of placement opportunities—one-eighth of the total annual ES placements in fiscal 1978—making CETA a very important source of business. It was apparent that if an ES agency wanted to stay competitive with other states and maintain its share of grant funds, that agency had to seek PSE placements.

LOCAL RECRUITMENT SYSTEMS

When the PSE expansion was announced in early 1977, sponsors had nearly 3 years of CETA experience. There were trained staffs, functioning organizations, and processes. Local CETA units had become accustomed to changing program requirements and expansions. By and large, local sponsors did not make wholesale changes in their organizational or recruitment systems when EJPEA was introduced. Such changes as did occur involved greater use of local organizations to recruit PSE participants and the use of the employment service to certify participant eligibility.

Sponsors normally manage PSE programs separately from other CETA programs and the recruitment processes differ. Only 4 of the sponsors in the study use a single recruitment system for all titles of CETA. Most sponsors (16 of 28) do use one recruitment system for the three PSE job programs (Title II, Title VI sustainment, and Title VI projects). Ten use one system for Title II and Title VI sustainment programs and another for PSE projects. The remaining two sponsors use a different system for each PSE program.

Although there are many variations in the handling of discrete recruitment activities, e.g., outreach, intake, screening, referral, eligibility certification, among local institutions studied, such activities fall into three patterns:

1. *Employment-service-centered*. The most common pattern, recruitment by the employment service, was used by most of the consortia (seven of the nine) and balance-of-state sponsors (three of four) in the study. Two of the four largest cities studied also preferred this arrangement. The employment service performs a range of intake functions along with eligibility verification. All potential participants are referred to the local ES office and are added to its list of people to be considered when filling PSE job orders. In several areas the employment service refers a potential enrollee not to an employer but to a CETA office or a central personnel office, which interviews applicants before they are sent to the selecting official of the employing agency. The intermediate interview permits the sponsor's CETA or personnel office to check vacancies and control referrals. Another reason for this step is local civil service requirements. If PSE slots are being filled under civil service procedures, the candidates are "tested" (usually a ranking based on education and experience) and placed on a register before being considered by the hiring official. A comparison of the characteristics of participants hired under the employment-service-centered pattern and the characteristics of participants hired under the sponsor-centered recruitment systems did not reveal any significant difference in the proportion of AFDC recipients, UI claimants, and veterans employed.

2. *Sponsor-centered* . Nine sponsors operate central intake units that interview and assess the needs of CETA applicants and make all referrals to PSE jobs and other CETA programs. Even where requests for PSE workers are sent to the local ES office, those referred (except veterans) are added to the list of eligible persons maintained by the central intake unit. This unit determines applicant eligibility and also ensures that the eligibility of an applicant for a Title VI project job is verified by the local ES office, either before or after the person is hired. Six of the nine counties in the study use this pattern.

3. *Employer-centered*. Sponsors using the employer-centered model delegate recruitment responsibilities to the PSE employer, who generally follows the same procedures he uses for hiring regular employees. The

employment service verifies the eligibility of applicants and assists in the recruitment of veterans and candidates for vacancies that are difficult to fill. Four of the seven sponsors using this pattern in fiscal 1976 dropped it in 1977. Three of the four went to the ES-centered system, and the fourth adopted the sponsor-centered design.

In addition to the new eligibility requirements, recruitment for projects was influenced by the policies of the prime sponsors in promoting and approving proposals. In half of the areas studied, the recruitment was applicant oriented. Prime sponsors advised eligible agencies to design projects compatible with the limited skills available among the long-term, low-income unemployed. This was often a consideration in the review of project proposals.

Although federal legislation was written from this "supply" standpoint, in the remaining half of the instances recruitment was "demand" oriented—that is, the job to be filled was of primary importance. The activity to be performed and the jobs to be filled were first determined. The skills necessary to perform the job were then identified, and finally a qualified candidate was selected.

The speed of the implementation and the short duration of projects made the use of an applicant-oriented system difficult, but that is not the only reason why job-oriented recruitment was common. Hiring agencies frequently viewed PSE programs as augmentations of ongoing activities and only secondarily as assistance to those who are at a disadvantage in competing for employment.

Once projects were approved, whether job- or applicant-oriented, PSE hiring paralleled regular hiring practices—the best available applicants were selected. Typically, several eligible persons from the pool were referred, and the employing agency selected the most qualified.

FINDING ELIGIBLE APPLICANTS

Almost all sponsors broadened their efforts to reach potential applicants in the 1977 expansion. This meant more extensive work with community groups that have direct contact with potential participants. Veteran organizations and welfare agencies were frequently added to a sponsor's list of screeners. The most intensive recruitment was conducted by the employment service. Local ES offices notified all UI claimants and WIN enrollees of their potential eligibility for Title VI jobs and requested them to come for interviews to determine their eligibility and availability.

Local officials pointed to the Department of Labor's hiring goal for veterans of 35 percent of new hires as a major factor that influenced the referral and hiring of participants (Table 11). As a consequence, the most active recruiting, including the little job development that did occur, was aimed at veterans. In a study conducted in 1977, Westat, Inc., found that 90 percent of 53 sponsors surveyed who engaged in recruitment made special efforts to attract veterans. Members of AFDC families were a distant second; 43 percent of the sponsors took some positive action to recruit AFDC recipients (Westat, Inc., 1978b, p. 28).

Stepped-up recruitment of all veterans increased their proportion in Title VI programs from 21 percent in the first half of fiscal 1977 to 29 percent of new enrollees in the second half. This, however, was followed by a decline to 23 percent for fiscal 1978. Although Vietnam veterans received particular attention, their representation in Title VI dropped from 8.7 percent in fiscal 1976 to 5.0 percent in 1978. There has been a gradual decrease in unemployed veterans who have served between 1964 and 1975. According to the Bureau of Labor Statistics the number of unemployed male Vietnam-era veterans between 20 and 34 years of age declined by 200,000 between the third quarter of calendar 1976 and the corresponding period of 1978. The unemployment rate for this group declined from 8.2 percent to 5.5 percent over this period. The unemployment rate for those between 20 and 24 years of age and for black males, however, was still more than twice as high as for all Vietnam-era veterans at that time.

The 28 survey areas reported similar trends. Eighteen areas showed decreases in the proportion of Title VI enrollees who were veterans between fiscal 1977 and 1978; 8 reported increases. In more than half of the sample areas, income and unemployment ineligibility were major reasons.[2]

The kinds of jobs available was another deterrent. In some instances they did not match the skills and experience of veterans; in other cases the salaries offered did not attract those veterans who had other income options. These findings are consistent with those reported in a Westat study. Although the number of cases examined is small, the study suggests that veterans had the highest rate of disinterest in PSE openings among several eligibility groups studied.

The impact of the new eligibility requirements is evident in the responses of local officials when asked to identify the most important factors influencing the selection of recruitment agencies (Table 12). The most often cited factor in choosing recruitment agencies was "access to desired client population." The influence of the ETA regional staff was cited almost as frequently. There are some notable differences among the

---

[2]Regulations exempt veterans from the unemployment requirement at the time of discharge, but the exemption does not apply for subsequent periods. GI benefits are not counted in computing family earnings, but veterans with working wives frequently could not qualify.

TABLE 11 Factors Identified by Local Officials as Having a Major Influence on the Hiring of Public Service Employment Participants, Sample Prime Sponsor Areas (percent of respondents)

Factor	Type of Respondent[a]			
	All Respondents	Prime Sponsor	Employment Service	Community-Based Organization
Applicant's qualifications for the job	84	88	79	83
Preference of employing agency for a particular individual	49	48	53	48
Targeting objectives of EJPEA	42	44	37	43
DOL veteran hiring goals	36	44	37	26
Compliance with affirmative action hiring goals	30	40	10	35
Local priorities for specific groups	12	12	10	13
Desire to minimize state or local welfare costs	12	12	10	0
Desire to reduce UI costs	10	8	26	4
Placement credit policies of DOL	7	4	21	4
Other	15	20	16	13
Number of respondents	(67)	(25)	(19)	(23)

[a] Columns add to more than 100 because of multiple factors cited.

answers of different groups responding to this question. Prime sponsors, which most frequently cited "access to desired client population," gave only slightly less emphasis to the past performance of the agencies doing PSE recruitment, the influence of ETA regional staff, and the sponsors' desire to control the PSE recruitment process. However, ETA regional staff most often cited their own influences and the regulation exempting sponsors from liability for ineligibles. Seventeen percent of the community-based respondents and 4 percent of the prime sponsors attributed the selection of recruitment agencies to "political" consideration.

Newspaper advertisements and articles about the new Title VI jobs were a widely used and effective means of attracting applicants. In some areas, ads were used to recruit applicants for hard-to-fill vacancies; in others, local policy required that all PSE jobs be publicly announced. Many sponsors planned no media efforts, but counted on disseminating information through regular local newspaper coverage. However originated, newspaper ads and stories consistently produced an ample supply of eligible candidates. One sponsor stopped using public advertisements to avoid raising hopes among persons not eligible. This sponsor found the new eligibility requirements difficult to communicate to job seekers, and, as a consequence, a third of those responding to PSE job publicity could not meet admission criteria.

DETERMINING AND VERIFYING ELIGIBILITY

Encouraged by the liability exemption for mispayments to ineligibles and pressured by ETA regional staff, all but two of the sponsors studied entered into formal agreements with employment service offices for eligibility determination. But sponsors did not necessarily leave all eligibility questions to the employment service. Many screened applicants thoroughly before sending them to the ES office. Employers and community groups also conducted preliminary eligibility screening before sending potential applicants to either the sponsor or the employment service. In most instances the only difference between the ES verification and the initial screening performed by the employer or community agency was that the ES action, usually involving a printed form, was considered the "official" and final determination of eligibility (Westat, Inc., 1978b, p. 32), since the employment service relied principally on the information provided and certified by the applicant.

In addition to determining the eligibility of the applicant, the employment service entered the applicant into the PSE pool and, if requested, referred the applicant back to the specific employer or the sponsor. If the applicant was hired, the ES was credited with a placement in its report to

TABLE 12 Factors Rated Important in Selection of Recruitment Agencies for Public Service Employment, Sample Prime Sponsor Areas (percent of respondents)

Reason for Selection	Type of Respondent					
	All Respondents[a]	Prime Sponsor	Employment Service	Community-Based Organization	Manpower Planning Council	Regional Office
Access to desired client population	42	50	59	30	30	41
Influence of ETA regional office	41	42	41	22	37	59
ETA regulations exempting sponsor from liability for ineligible participants if eligibility is verified by ES	33	38	30	30	30	37
Desire to control PSE recruitment process	32	42	37	26	26	26
Past performance of agency doing PSE recruitment	24	46	26	13	18	15
Timing of PSE expansion	16	35	15	0	15	15
Cost	10	23	4	0	15	7
Political considerations	9	4	11	17	4	11
Number of respondents	(130)	(26)	(27)	(23)	(27)	(27)

[a] Columns add to more than 100 because of multiple factors cited.

ETA. In several areas, this determination and referral was performed by ES staff located in the sponsor's central intake unit.

For the most part, changes in recruitment practices resulting from the new eligibility requirements did not appear to decrease duplication between the employment service and the sponsors nor to increase the coordination between various recruitment efforts within the CETA program or among local institutions. Of 17 field observers noting a change, 9 reported more duplication of activities in determining eligibility, and 8 reported less. The ES review often formalized what a preliminary screener had recorded.

In addition, the ETA policy of permitting postentry verification was not as helpful as it appeared to be. It is extremely awkward to terminate someone already hired, particularly because of a requirement unrelated to job qualifications or performance. To avoid this, sponsors ordinarily closely reviewed the eligibility of participants who were hired before receiving the ES formal verification. As a result, the participant's postentry trip to the ES local office for verification of eligibility was mostly for the record.

The extreme pressure to meet the DOL hiring schedules discouraged prime sponsors from taking the time necessary to perform thorough eligibility checks. It also led prime sponsors to advertise Title VI jobs, which often attracted persons not eligible for the program and encouraged preselection. All of this adversely affected the accomplishment of EJPEA's targeting objective.

A variant of the eligibility verification problem occurs when persons reported a change in their residence, family, or labor force status for the purpose of meeting the eligibility requirements. The more attractive the job, the more common this practice is likely to be.

EMPLOYMENT SERVICE POOLS

A nationally developed concept can be modified, misinterpreted, and even ignored at the implementation level. Whatever the intent of its framers, a national directive filters through the interests and biases of regional and local officials. Implementation is molded by the traditions, practices, and relationships among institutions and officials as well as by particular local needs. Out of this adaptation process many local variations of the central design emerge. What happened to the concept of the ES pool illustrates this.

In planning for the PSE expansion, local sponsors and ES offices were told by ETA officials to develop procedures jointly to establish "pools" of potentially eligible UI and WIN enrollees by March 1, 1977.

Nineteen of the sponsors in the study used an ES pool; two also operated duplicate pools, and in another jurisdiction a community-based organization ran a duplicate pool. In five areas, the sponsor rather than the employment service maintained and operated the pool. In four instances, the sponsor did not use a pool. In some areas, ES staff located in the sponsor's central intake unit registered and verified "walk-ins." The process was reversed in one area, where sponsor staff were stationed in the local ES office. Where relationships between the sponsor and the employment service had been smooth in the past, the pool concept worked reasonably well. Where relationships had been poor, the pool never realized its potential in contributing to the PSE buildup and tended to fall apart quickly.

Some of the problems in setting up and maintaining pools were lack of information on the characteristics of the labor supply, difficulty in contacting potentially eligible persons, communication problems between the employment service and prime sponsor offices, and allegations of delays in referral of applicants.

While the pool was a useful method for quickly identifying an initial group of persons eligible for new jobs, it was an arrangement that could not long endure. Maintaining current information for a long list of eligible persons and attempting to screen such a list to fill specific job orders was awkward and time-consuming. In addition, the ES listing, which included mainly UI and WIN eligibles, comprised only part of the eligible group. Sponsors reported a heavy flow of "walk-in" applicants, particularly after publicity on PSE jobs, and they were obliged to consider the eligible persons in this group as well as UI and WIN enrollees. As a result, sponsors with central intake units maintained their own pool of eligibles, to which they added the candidates referred by the employment service, or they maintained and operated the pools themselves. Given the time and effort necessary to maintain the pools, it is not surprising that the system quickly fell apart once sponsors found they had little difficulty locating a ready supply of eligibles.

There is, however, one aspect of the pool that could be valuable to CETA planners. The ES pool was a potential source of information about the characteristics and skills of the eligible population in a sponsor area. On the basis of such information, sponsors can inform agencies designing projects of the skills available so that project activities can make the most effective use of persons eligible to participate. However, information on the characteristics of persons in the pool was seldom well developed.

MEETING HIRING SCHEDULES

Only one sponsor in the study had serious difficulty in identifying sufficient eligibles to meet hiring goals. The ES pools of UI claimants and WIN participants were immediately available, and large numbers of ready and eager job seekers responded to news stories. Failure to meet hiring schedules stemmed from procedural delays in establishing and describing jobs and in processing a larger number of projects and applicants than some systems or staffs could handle in the time allotted. Delays also occurred in some areas because projects called for skills which were not available in the pool of eligible participants. A CETA administrator commented that at one time one-third of all approved project jobs could not be filled because the skills wanted were not available in the pool.

Hiring schedules were the overriding concern of sponsors. The necessity to meet schedules was constantly emphasized by ETA staff, who hovered closely over local operations, threatening to withdraw funds if goals were not met. This emphasis on speed had both positive and negative effects. Seeking ways to quicken the hiring pace, many sponsors chose projects and jobs that could easily be filled by unskilled workers—those who most needed assistance in the labor market. On the other hand, some sponsors abandoned normal recruitment processes and controls. Employers were encouraged to seek out anyone who could be cleared quickly. This often led to the employment of either "preselected" or ineligible participants. In addition, there was often a mismatch between applicant and job. Too often the first "warm body" who came in the door was hired. Although these quick marriages served to fill job slots, they frequently resulted in unhappy participants and employers, who soon parted company.

During the last quarter of fiscal 1977, some 80,000 participants left Title VI jobs, while 227,000 were hired. In the first quarter of fiscal 1978, over 80,000 left and 152,000 were hired. The data do not indicate what proportion of the terminations were persons recently hired, but observers report that many of the new participants stayed only briefly. Only one-third of those leaving Title VI jobs in the last quarter of fiscal 1977 went on to other jobs; in fiscal 1978 slightly less (30 percent) obtained other employment.

MATCHING JOBS AND ELIGIBLE APPLICANTS

Although the total number of eligible applicants was adequate, the majority of sponsors in the study (18 of 28) reported difficulties in matching eligible applicants with approved jobs. One reported a problem locating arrestfree applicants for a parapolice program. Almost all had difficulty in recruiting supervisory personnel and filling jobs requiring extensive qualifications or experience. The cause of the problem differed with the perspective of those who viewed it. Job interviewers in ES local offices or sponsor intake units thought employers were asking for the impossible. Employers, on the other hand, thought the new CETA eligibility requirements were arbitrary and restrictive and that the $10,000 wage limit made it difficult to hire for some jobs, especially for supervisors.

Under the pressures of meeting hiring schedules, sponsors did not let jobs remain vacant for long and forced employers to accommodate themselves to the qualifications of the applicants. Inability to find qualified applicants for a PSE job usually led to lowering the qualifications for the job or restructuring the job to make it easier to fill. If the employer was unwilling to do either, efforts to fill the job were abandoned. CETA staff concentrated on jobs they believed had a better chance of being filled. In some instances, a job was cancelled when an employer was unable to select one of a limited number of applicants sent for interview. Less-often-used methods for handling hard-to-fill vacancies were to widen the applicant search, sometimes even advertising for applicants.

There are differing views as to whether the difficulties in matching jobs with eligible participants will continue and increase. One local observer notes that, as PSE jobs are filled with the most qualified and experienced applicants, the size of this group quickly diminishes and matching worker to job becomes more difficult. Another's more optimistic view is that sponsors are changing their approach to Title VI projects. As sponsors learn more about the people eligible, they become more sensitive to their limitations and more carefully review project plans to ensure that there are eligible candidates before jobs are approved. This change to more "applicant-oriented" programs would lessen the job–man match problems.

REFERRING APPLICANTS TO EMPLOYERS

The ways that sponsors find applicants and refer them to employers are governed as much by chance as by design. Eligible candidates are matched with jobs on the basis of three elements: the vacancies to be filled, the skills required to fill those vacancies, and the qualifications of the applicants available. None of the sponsors and only a few ES local offices now have the computer capability to store and retrieve applicant and job data quickly. The job–man match is limited to the applicants known to the interviewer filling the job order. Normally the most common matches are with the applicants most recently interviewed and remembered.

Although congressional focus was on the eligible applicants, sponsor concerns were often job-oriented. There was little effort on the part of the sponsors studied to go beyond the normal referral process and give special consideration to a specific group or type of applicant, except for veterans.

The reports of the field research associates indicate that most sponsors did not establish a system to ensure the equitable allocation of PSE resources among the four categories of eligibles; in some cases sponsors were not even aware of the congressional directive to establish such a mechanism. Out of the 27 sample sponsors for which data was available, 16 made no attempt to allocate jobs in light of the composition of the eligible population. Five sponsors made some attempt, usually informally, to monitor the allocation of jobs among the categories of eligible persons. Only 6 sponsors had systems whereby the proportion of jobs allocated to a category of eligible persons could be adjusted to conform with an estimate of the composition of the eligible population.

Prime sponsor administrators cited a number of reasons for not establishing a mechanism for monitoring the allocation of jobs by category of eligibility. Many noted that in the rush to meet the hiring quota there was not time to be concerned with which segment of the eligible population a particular applicant was drawn from.

Other sponsors questioned the importance of the equity requirement. If a person met the eligibility requirements, wasn't that enough? Still other sponsors suggested that goals, such as 35 percent veteran participation, had taken precedence over attempting to ensure an equitable allocation of jobs.

Inadequate data on the composition of the eligible population was also frequently cited as a barrier to allocating PSE resources in light of the composition of the population of eligible persons. Although ES local offices collected data on the eligible applicants in the PSE pools, these often served areas larger than those of the sponsors' jurisdictions, and they usually could not accurately disaggregate what data they did collect. All sponsors reported that they reviewed participant characteristics after hiring, but none identified the criteria they used to evaluate hiring results or indicate whether their evaluations had led to specific hiring adjustments.

With the implementation of the EJPEA, there was for the first time a real difference between Title II and Title VI jobs. There can be a substantial money and career difference between referral to a Title II and a Title VI project job; one has an indefinite duration, the other is part of a short-term project. There are also great variations in wages for the same jobs within a sponsor's area and among projects. However, none of the sponsors in the study had policies for assigning eligibles to the three PSE job categories. The decision as to whether an applicant, eligible for all three programs, is assigned to a Title II, Title VI sustainment, or Title VI project job appears to be based solely upon the interviewer's knowledge of current vacancies.

No formal guidelines have been issued by ETA to ensure impartial selection of applicants.

Another factor to be considered in the selection of applicants is the local merit system. Many have been modified to allow PSE jobs to be limited to those that meet federally established eligibility requirements. Candidates are ranked on the basis of qualifications and experience; those at the top of the list are referred to the selecting official. Including PSE participants in merit system procedures facilitates the transition of the participants to a regular permanent job if an unsubsidized position becomes available. There is, however, a trade-off. It limits the sponsors' ability to give preference to specific groups—AFDC recipients, minorities, or other categories that the sponsor has identified as a significant segment of the unemployed population needing special assistance.

EMPLOYMENT DECISIONS

The pool of persons eligible for Title VI under the revised criteria was about 10 times larger than the number of jobs available. The question of who among the eligible population should be hired was left to the discretion of the local officials. Although project design and approval was influenced in half of the areas by expectations that the bulk of the persons eligible to participate would have few skills, once projects were approved the participant selection process was job oriented.

Selection is summed up by one CETA administrator as follows: "(1) clients must be willing to work; (2) they must be 'clean cut' and neat; and (3) they must have a skill that can be matched with a job." Local officials and staff of sponsors, the employment service, and community-based organizations reported that the individual's qualifications for the job were most often the deciding factor in selection (Table 11). Eighty-four percent of these officials cited "qualifications" as a major influence in hiring decisions. The preference of the employing agency for a particular individual was the second most important factor, followed by the targeting objectives of EJPEA and the DOL hiring goals for veterans. This selection preference illustrates the divergence between national policy, which emphasized helping those most in need, and the preferences of local hiring agencies for those whom they judge best qualified of those eligible for PSE nonsustainment positions. Differences in responses by class of respondents are also revealing. Employment service officials, for example, tended to cite reductions in welfare and unemployment insurance costs as important considerations, while community-based organizations stressed affirmative action goals.

When asked why applicants accepted PSE jobs, 82 percent of these officials agreed that applicants preferred working to not working, and 77 percent believed they were attracted by the prospect of increased income (Table 13). Their perceptions of why applicants rejected PSE jobs covered a variety of factors: too low wages; not interested in the skills or occupations of the PSE jobs; and the short duration of PSE jobs (Table 14). However, jobs were seldom rejected.

There is a difference of opinion on these responses. Sponsor staff, for example, were more likely than union officials to believe that some PSE applicants accepted PSE positions for fear of being disqualified for welfare or UI benefits. Nearly half of the sponsor staffs interviewed indicated that transportation or day care problems were reasons for rejecting PSE positions, but none of the union respondents agreed.

A Westat study conducted during the PSE buildup indicates the varying interest in PSE jobs among the eligible participants. The number of cases was limited, but they do show that eligible veterans were more likely to drop out of consideration for a PSE job due to lack of interest than any other group of participants. They had a 9 percent dropout rate (failed to report for interview, refused job, or failed to report to work). UI claimants had the next highest drop rate (7.3 percent), followed by persons who had exhausted their UI benefits (4.7 percent), AFDC family members (3.2 percent), and other unemployed persons not eligible for UI (2.9 percent) (Westat, 1978a, pp. 43–45).

One consideration in accepting or refusing a PSE job is the financial incentive for those receiving income transfer payments (Aid to Families with Dependent Children or unemployment insurance). Decisions will be made on the basis of net advantages, that is, the PSE wage, plus any utility gained by working, minus alternative payments and utility derived from leisure lost by accepting the PSE job. For transfer recipients, the high implicit tax rate to their alternative earning should they return to work may make PSE jobs relatively less profitable. Variations in payments from locality to locality make it difficult to generalize or to estimate the extent to which financial incentives enter into the decision of transfer payment recipients to accept or reject a PSE job. The General Accounting Office compared the income from a PSE job with UI and AFDC direct cash benefits in eight sponsor areas. After considering average wages and the loss or retention of cash benefits, the GAO found that net quantifiable incentives to accept a PSE job ranged from $1.46 to $1.60 an hour for AFDC recipients and from $1.36 an hour to a loss of $.48 an hour for UI claimants. However, these computations did not include significant job costs such as transportation, clothing, and meals, or the value of loss of AFDC-related benefits such as Medicaid and child care (U.S. General Accounting Office, 1978, pp. 21–32).

TABLE 13 Perceptions of Local Officials of Reasons Individuals Accept Public Service Employment Positions, Sample Prime Sponsor Areas (percent of respondents)

Reason for Acceptance	Type of Respondent[a]					
	All Respondents	Prime Sponsor	Employment Service	Community-Based Organization	Nonprofit Organizations	Unions
Prefer working to not working	82	81	85	92	71	79
Increased income	77	89	85	69	71	68
Opportunity to acquire new skill	34	48	37	27	29	26
Fringe benefits (i.e., health insurance)	20	22	18	12	17	37
Risk of disqualification for UI	13	22	15	12	12	0
Risk of reduction in food stamps or welfare benefits	8	15	7	4	8	5
Other	11	18	11	12	8	5
Number of respondents	(123)	(27)	(27)	(26)	(24)	(19)

[a] Columns add to more than 100 because of multiple factors cited.

TABLE 14 Perceptions of Local Officials of Reasons Individuals Do Not Accept Public Service Employment Positions, Sample Prime Sponsor Areas (percent of respondents)

Reason for Not Accepting Position	Type of Respondent[a]					
	All Respondents	Prime Sponsor	Employment Service	Community-Based Organization	Nonprofit Organizations	Unions
PSE wages too low compared to alternative income sources (i.e., UI, welfare)	35	52	38	38	21	14
Interest in a particular skill or occupational area other than that available through Title II or VI	33	48	25	42	16	28
Transportation or child care problems	32	48	29	38	32	0
PSE too short term	31	32	42	29	32	14
Lack of interest in working	19	20	21	25	5	21
Reduction in income from previous position or compared to UI or welfare benefits	18	20	29	17	5	14
Loss in status or money associated with a Title II or VI job compared to previous position	17	20	29	17	5	7
Poor health/physical requirements of job	12	16	21	8	5	7
Desire to return to work for former employer	11	16	12	12	5	7
Other	12	24	4	12	10	7
Number of respondents	(106)	(25)	(24)	(24)	(19)	(14)

[a] Columns add to more than 100 because of multiple factors cited.

PRESELECTION, PATRONAGE, AND INELIGIBILITY

Filling jobs in the public sector through political patronage has a long history. Where they exist, merit systems have generally restricted the practice, although it occasionally flourishes in informal systems. The PSE program, despite congressional stipulations, has not been completely immune, particularly where PSE jobs are outside the merit system. Note that there is a "trade-off" between the advantages of the merit system in controlling patronage and its tendency to select those most likely to succeed rather than those most in need. Persons coming through merit systems also have a greater likelihood of being "transitioned" into a regular public service job.

As the PSE program doubled during the summer and fall of 1977, allegations of political influence and patronage cropped up across the country. The Department of Labor, sometimes joined by the Department of Justice, had investigations under way in a dozen areas. A few field observers noted that political influence affected hiring in the sponsor areas they studied. In one area, an observer found it very commonand that sponsor was under investigation by the Department of Labor. A second observer reported sporadic use of political influence in hiring. In four other areas isolated instances of political referral occurred.

The creation of jobs for specific individuals or manipulation of the recruiting and referral system to hire preselected participants was reported in 16 of the 28 sponsor areas in the study. As with patronage, the actual incidence is difficult to determine precisely or even to estimate. Preselection, too, is an informal, undocumented technique used in both the private and public job sectors. Unemployed individuals, as well as employed individuals seeking a job change, make extensive use of job information and assistance from family, friends, and acquaintances. Along with information, friends and family provide references and endorsements that often carry weight with a selecting official who would prefer to pick someone endorsed by a person he or she trusts.

Although the use of information and endorsements by friends and family is generally appropriate in the private sector, it is questionable in a public jobs program. Congress intended that federally funded jobs should be equally accessible to all eligible persons in the target groups. Federal regulations gave this policy substance by requiring sponsors to use open and objective methods to select participants. Some sponsors do have rigorous controls to guard against preselection and stiffly resist it, as they do political referrals. Others accept preselection as a normal part of the employment process. At times sponsors have even fostered it as an expedient method to fill jobs and meet hiring schedules—their overriding concern. Field observers note that the new eligibility requirements have made preselection more difficult and have reduced its incidence.

Strict application of eligibility requirements is difficult and the process prone to error and fraud. Yet the lack of adequate eligibility verification reduced the effect of the EJPEA criteria. The difficulty of ensuring ready program access to the eligible, while safeguarding against the entry of the ineligible, is evident in both the welfare and unemployment compensation programs. Nevertheless, this area was not sufficiently addressed in planning for PSE. ETA regulations under EJPEA left responsibility for applicant eligibility dangling between the sponsor and the employment service. Neither was liable for error as long as there was a formal agreement requiring the employment service to verify the eligibility of applicants. The results are reported in two studies conducted during the peak of the expansion. Westat, Inc., in reviewing local processes, experienced "considerable difficulty in developing estimates (for screening and verification of participant eligibility) . . . as records were frequently of questionable accuracy and infrequently nonexistent" (Westat, Inc., 1978b, p. 29). The Department of Labor auditors found that procedures for assessing participant eligibility needed improvement because "most sponsors have not designed application forms which provide sufficient information to determine eligibility; do not require participants to provide documentation; and do not have adequate procedures for verifying information and applications" (U.S. Department of Labor, 1978, p. 5).

In its study of participant eligibility, Department of Labor audit staff found that 12 percent of the participants in the sample reviewed were either ineligible (9.8 percent) or that there was insufficient information to make a determination of eligibility (2.5 percent). Of the 131 ineligibles who received jobs, 55 had neither met the criteria for the long-term unemployed nor for AFDC family members; 36 had family incomes exceeding the minimum income level; 27 had jobs at the time of application; and 5 had obtained full-time jobs after application but before the PSE job offer. The auditors found that the ineligible rate under the new criteria was almost twice that under the old requirements (U.S. Department of Labor, 1978). Data from Westat's Continuous Longitudinal Manpower Survey indicated that the ineligibility rate may be double that found by the Department of Labor auditors. Of the 146,000 Title VI enrollees subject to the new eligibility requirements hired during the last half of fiscal 1977, 25 percent appeared to be ineligible. Thirteen percent had family incomes greater than 70 percent of the BLS lower living standard, 3 percent had been unemployed less than 15 of the 20 weeks prior to entry into the program, and 9 percent appeared to meet neither the family income nor long-term unemployed criteria.[3]

CONCLUSION

The next chapter analyzes the effect of EJPEA targeting criteria on the participants of public service employment programs. But as the foregoing discussion shows, local hiring practices have tended to minimize the effects in several ways. While the new criteria narrowed the eligibility for participation in PSE programs, nationally there were still 10 eligible persons for every job, a fact that allowed local programs wide choice in hiring. Their selection processes illustrate the divergence between the national policy emphasis on helping those most in need and the preferences of local agencies for workers with the best record of education and experience.

The more restrictive eligibility requirements and sponsor actions in half the areas to stimulate projects for workers with few skills created more job opportunities for the disadvantaged. After projects were approved, however, sponsor choices reveal a pattern of job-oriented hiring. The pressure to meet hiring goals forced many prime sponsors to accede to the preference of the employing agencies. As a result, participants were referred and selected on the basis of suitability for a particular job. The emphasis placed on meeting the hiring schedule occasionally led to the practice of allowing hiring agencies to preselect individuals for hard-to-fill orders. Finally, there was little evidence that prime sponsors took seriously the requirement for equitable service to members of families receiving AFDC, persons receiving unemployment insurance benefits, and other low-income, long-term unemployed.

Inadequate eligibility verification was another factor that reduced the impact of the EJPEA targeting criteria. The EJPEA criteria, especially the family income requirement, were difficult to verify. In many cases, the applicant's interview responses had to suffice. Second, sponsors were encouraged to avoid liability for ineligible participants by using the ES to certify eligibility. Since the ES was no better equipped than the prime sponsor to check on the applicant's family income, the result was simply to eliminate any accountability for ineligibles. Indeed, incentives for the ES, which was not financially liable for errors in certification, may run in the direction of maximizing PSE referrals and placements. For the ES, placements are the "coin of the realm," since they are a major factor in determining local budgets.

[3]Based on preliminary unpublished data from the Continuous Longitudinal Manpower Survey (Westat, Inc.).

Given the complexity of the criteria and the problems of eligibility verification, it is not surprising that a significant portion of the Title VI participants hired under EJPEA were ineligible in areas examined by DOL auditors. Since ineligible participants come disproportionately from the better qualified segment of the PSE pool, poor verification procedures erode the effectiveness of the EJPEA targeting criteria as a means of shifting the PSE program toward the structurally unemployed, transfer payment recipients, and others most in need.

A third factor tending to reduce the impact of the EJPEA eligibility criteria is the participation incentive structure. Some eligible individuals with other alternatives have less incentive to seek PSE jobs than others. For example, an AFDC recipient with very limited skills may prefer to remain on AFDC rather than take a low wage PSE job. Persons receiving UI benefits will also weigh their opportunity costs.

This may create a dilemma: While a high PSE wage will encourage transfer recipients to take jobs, it will also attract better qualified individuals both in and out of the eligible pool. This is likely to reduce the proportion of needy persons in the program. Conversely, if the PSE wage structure is low only those persons with few alternatives (those most in need) will be attracted to PSE jobs. However, given a choice, it is likely that transfer payment recipients will choose not to accept low-wage PSE jobs.

The participant incentive structure thus can significantly affect the participation of certain groups in the PSE program. To the extent that the incentive structure introduces a systematic bias against participation by some segments of the eligible pool, it reduces the targeting criteria's effectiveness.

6 Program Participants

One of the principal objectives of the Emergency Jobs Programs Extension Act (EJPEA) was to target a larger proportion of public service employment (PSE) to jobs for the most needy of the unemployed. This chapter assesses the extent to which this objective was achieved. In brief it finds that:

1. The tighter eligibility requirements of EJPEA reduced the number of persons eligible for the newly created PSE positions (Title VI, nonsustainment) and increased the proportion of disadvantaged participants in these jobs. But the impact upon the total PSE program was offset by several developments.

  a. Because EJPEA targeted only a portion of the PSE jobs to the disadvantaged, prime sponsors were able to change the mix of participants in other programs.

  b. Employing agencies tended to preselect candidates and to hire the best qualified individuals from the eligible population.

  c. The absence of an effective eligibility verification system led to the enrollment of a significant number of ineligible participants.

2. Under these circumstances, the overall characteristics profile of PSE participants changed very little, although there was a significant increase in the proportion of persons with family incomes below the poverty level.

WHO SHOULD BE SERVED? STRADDLING THE ISSUES

From the time that public service employment programs were enacted in the early 1970s, there has been considerable ambivalence about the clientele to be served. Typically, job creation legislation had been directed toward the cyclically unemployed, although concern has also been expressed for the structurally unemployed—persons who have the most difficulty in the job market, even in periods of low employment. The statutes' eligibility provisions gave all unemployed persons access to the programs, although the rhetoric of the legislation was directed to the special problems of the disadvantaged.

The Emergency Employment Act of 1971 was designed to counter a rise in unemployment and was intended broadly for the "unemployed and underemployed" population, regardless of family income or duration of unemployment.[1] However, the act's preamble suggests that Congress was especially concerned with those in the labor market who are handicapped by structural difficulties, such as the low-income unemployed, migrant workers, recently separated veterans, and new entrants into the labor force. Prime sponsors were required to give preference to persons in these categories. The EEA also required that the "significant segments" (locally defined groups most in need of help) of the unemployed population be served equitably, to the extent possible. This "equitable service" concept was later incorporated into CETA.

When Congress enacted CETA in 1973, it included a vestige of the EEA in Title II, which provided for a modest (50,000 positions) PSE program in areas of substantial unemployment (6.5 percent). In this respect, the program was directed to the structural problems of particular geographic areas. But Title II also had structural overtones in terms of the people it was to serve. Sponsors were to give "consideration" to unemployed persons "who are most seriously disadvantaged in terms of the length of time they have been unemployed and their prospect of finding employment without assistance." Despite this admonition, participation in CETA public service jobs was in fact open to a broader group—all persons who were unemployed 30 days or more or who were underemployed. Thus, Title II straddled the structural/countercyclical issue. Although it urged that special consideration be given to the structurally unemployed, the legislation in fact gave local sponsors wide discretion in selecting PSE participants.

The Emergency Jobs and Unemployment Assistance Act, passed at a

---

[1]Subsequent DOL regulations did require a 14-day period of unemployment.

time of soaring unemployment, established Title VI in CETA and authorized $2.5 billion to subsidize 300,000 temporary public service jobs for the unemployed. The effect of this large new program was to shift the emphasis of CETA from the Title I employability development programs to a countercyclical PSE program for persons rendered jobless by the recession of 1974. The only hard eligibility requirement for jobs in Title VI was that the participant be unemployed or underemployed. "Preferred consideration" was to be given to those who had exhausted their UI entitlement (or who were not eligible for UI), as well as those out of work for 15 weeks or longer. But, again, the act stopped short of mandating an eligibility requirement for the long-term, low-income unemployed.

In sum, early PSE programs were characterized by indecision—specific language of the legislation directing the programs to the cyclically unemployed was accompanied by general expressions of concern for the structurally unemployed.

The varying cyclical/structural emphases in manpower programs reflect the state of the labor market, as well as the debate on the role of PSE in manpower policy. When unemployment is high, the focus tends to be on unemployed persons generally. At relatively low levels of unemployment, attention reverts to the structurally unemployed. The phase of a recession is particularly relevant to the kinds of participants who are enrolled in public service employment programs. At its onset, the countercyclical effect of PSE is not significantly affected by the kinds of unemployed persons admitted into the program. However, at the recovery stage, who is enrolled may be quite significant, since the employment of skilled workers in subsidized public sector jobs may tend to contribute to shortages in the private sector.

THE EMERGENCY JOBS PROGRAMS EXTENSION ACT

The Emergency Jobs Programs Extension Act (EJPEA) for the first time reserved a major portion of PSE jobs for the structurally unemployed. The new PSE positions made available by the Economic Stimulus Appropriations Act of 1976 and half of the vacancies that occur in the sponsors' sustainment levels are limited to the long-term low-income unemployed and AFDC recipients.[2]

EJPEA's targeting criteria were a response to what Congress perceived as one of the deficiencies in the CETA Title VI program—inadequate participation of the disadvantaged. Prior to its passage, the majority of

[2]The sustainment level is defined as the number of Title VI positions as of June 1976 or October 1976, whichever was higher in a prime sponsor area.

participants in Title VI did not have incomes below the poverty level, less than half were unemployed prior to entry into the program, and most of those who were unemployed had been jobless less than 15 weeks. Only 6 percent were AFDC recipients, and 14 percent were unemployment insurance beneficiaries at the time of enrollment. In the main, they were white men with at least a high school education.[3]

The relatively well-paying jobs in the PSE programs of Titles II and VI were serving persons much more able to compete in the regular job market than those served in programs provided under Title I. Enrollees in Title II and Title VI were much more likely to be male, white, and have post-high-school education and were less likely to be members of families receiving AFDC or be hindered by a specific employment barrier such as limited English or a police record.

By tightening the eligibility requirements for most of the Title VI jobs, Congress sought (a) to ensure that more public service jobs would be directed to the most needy and (b) to shift the costs of transfer payment programs such as unemployment insurance and Aid to Families with Dependent Children to a program that placed beneficiaries in productive jobs. The Senate report (U.S. Congress, 1976c, p. 17) states these objectives directly:

A basic purpose of the Committee bill's provision is to attempt to distribute a limited number of jobs—in view of the 7 million individuals officially counted as unemployed—among those whose financial need for these jobs is the greatest and among those who are receiving federal, state, and local cash payments either from unemployment compensation or public assistance. It makes less sense to continue to provide cash payments to individuals who are not working than to find productive jobs in our communities.

The Senate committee report pointed out that more than 2 million persons were expected to exhaust their entitlement to unemployment compensation in 1976. Due to the severity of the 1975 recession, Congress had already extended the duration of unemployment insurance benefits twice. Rather than repeat this process and shift an even greater portion of the UI system's costs to the federal level, Congress chose to make PSE jobs available to those persons whose unemployment insurance benefits had ended.

In addition to expressed congressional intent, there were other reasons for reorienting the public service employment program toward the

---

[3]Data on CETA participants who formerly received unemployment insurance are from Employment and Training Administration program reports. All other data are from the Continuous Longitudinal Manpower Survey (Westat, Inc., 1977, Tables 5-4, 5-14, 6-1, and 6-2).

structurally unemployed. These became relevant as the economy recovered. It was thought that a large-scale countercyclical program, open to all jobless people, might compete with private enterprise for skilled labor—bidding up wages and thus contributing to inflation. By ensuring that only the structurally unemployed had access to public service employment jobs, this possibility was minimized.

EJPEA altered Title VI eligibility requirements in three ways. It extended the required duration of unemployment from 30 days to 15 weeks. It introduced an income standard; eligibility for most new PSE openings required that a person's family income had to be below the BLS low-income standard or the poverty level, depending on which was higher.[4] It identified four categories of the low-income unemployed and required that PSE jobs be allocated equitably among them. Each of the categories—AFDC recipients, UI beneficiaries for 15 weeks or more, UI exhaustees, and other low-income persons unemployed for 15 weeks or more—was to be served " . . . in light of the population of the categories of eligible unemployed persons within the prime sponsor's area" (U.S. Congress, 1976c, p. 18). The conference report noted that, while sponsors might lack data on the number of eligible persons in each category, Congress intended that they make a "good faith" effort to meet this requirement (U.S. Congress, 1976b, p. 17).

Most of the respondents interviewed in the study believed that the eligibility standards of EJPEA introduced a finer mesh for screening persons most in need than the looser criteria applicable to Title II and to half of the sustainment positions. However, some believed the criteria were too restrictive, and others thought that they were not restrictive enough. Some sponsors, particularly those in urban areas, felt that the income criterion was too low, chiefly because it was based on total family income. With family income as the standard, it was difficult, where the head of the household was employed, for other wage earners in a family to qualify, and in some instances unemployed heads of families were ineligible because another person in the family was employed.

Those who believed the income criterion was too high pointed out that annualizing incomes based on the latest 3 months permits persons with relatively high earnings during the rest of the year to qualify on an equal basis with those with much less income.

There was even greater concern about the 15-week unemployment

---

[4]In 1977, for a family of four, 70 percent of the BLS lower living standard averaged $6,871. The poverty level was $5,675. However, for smaller family units, the poverty level sometimes exceeded the 70 percent level.

standard, which tends to exclude seasonally or intermittently employed low-income persons who cannot "afford" to be unemployed for 15 weeks.

Although sponsors prefer to enroll heads of households in PSE programs, it is more difficult for a person in a multiworker family to meet the family income requirement. For this reason, the eligibility criteria favor single-member families. Indeed, there are indications that persons interested in participating in PSE programs may be establishing themselves as single-member families in order to qualify. In the last half of fiscal 1977, after the EJPEA criteria went into effect, the proportion of Title VI enrollees who were classified as one-person families rose sharply, according to preliminary CLMS data.

Emphasis on the long-term unemployed and low-income population has now been built into CETA through the Comprehensive Employment and Training Act Amendments of 1978. This reauthorization act attempts to resolve the structural/countercyclical dilemma by establishing two distinct PSE programs: a continuing program to provide public service jobs to the disadvantaged (Title II, Part D) and a program for the cyclically unemployed funded on a contingency basis (Title VI).[5]

WHO IS SERVED? THE IMPACT OF EJPEA ELIGIBILITY CRITERIA

Since resources to fund PSE positions are inadequate to absorb even a modest proportion of the unemployed, it is necessary to determine which groups in the unemployed population are to be served and to limit, through eligibility requirements, program access to these groups.

Congress was unwilling to subject all of Title VI to the new criteria because it would disrupt existing PSE programs and would be unacceptable to most prime sponsors, who were insisting on local flexibility. A middle course was chosen. The new criteria were to apply to the new project positions created by the expansion of Title VI (nonsustainment). Title VI positions as of June 1976 (sustainment) would only be affected as vacancies occurred.[6] Half of these replacements would have to meet the new eligibility criteria.

[5]One of the anomalies resulting from EJPEA was its effect on the distinction between Titles II and VI. Title II, originally intended for the disadvantaged long-term unemployed, was subject to less stringent eligibility requirements than Title VI, the countercyclical program.

[6]Sponsors were allowed to fund sustainment Title VI jobs up to the level of June 1976 or October 1976, whichever was higher.

CHANGES IN THE SIZE AND COMPOSITION OF THE ELIGIBLE
POPULATION

By March 1978, there were 347,000 new Title VI project positions
(nonsustainment) and 266,000 sustainment positions, as shown in Table
15. Approximately 31 percent of sustainment Title VI participants should
have met the new targeting criteria as of that date.[7] On balance, out of a
total of 742,000 participants enrolled in Titles II and VI in March 1978, 58
percent were hired under the new admission requirements. The remaining
42 percent were hired under the pre-EJPEA eligibility requirements.

EJPEA drastically tightened eligibility for Title VI jobs and increased
significantly the proportion of disadvantaged individuals in the eligible
population. Prior to EJPEA, about 20 million persons were eligible for
286,000 Title VI jobs (Table 16). After EJPEA, 4.4 million met the new
requirements for the expansion positions and half of the vacancies in the
sustainment level. Thus, the size of the eligible population was reduced by
more than 75 percent.

Not only the size, but also the characteristics, of the eligible population
were affected by EJPEA (see Table 16). Reflecting congressional targeting
objectives, reductions in the number of eligible persons were concentrated
among the better educated white males with incomes above the poverty
level. As a result, the proportion of economically disadvantaged eligibles
increased 51 percentage points and the proportion of persons with less
than a high school education rose by 14 points. The proportion of
nonwhites nearly doubled and substantial increases were reported for
women. On the other hand, the proportion of persons of prime working
age increased 13 percentage points.

The overall changes in the size and composition of the eligible
population conform closely to the congressional intent to serve the
financially needy and those receiving income support. Nearly all of the

---

[7]This estimate represents the proportion of participants that should have met the new
targeting criteria based on the following length-of-stay estimates:

Proportion of Total Enrollees Terminating in:

More than 12 months	47 percent
9–12 months	5 percent
6–9 months	10 percent
3–6 months	20 percent
Less than 3 months	18 percent

These length of stay estimates are based on data collected by the Continuous Longitudinal
Manpower Survey pertaining to the January to June 1975 cohort of PSE enrollees (Westat,
Inc., 1978a, p. 5-31).

TABLE 15　CETA Public Service Employment Program Participants, March 1978, by Eligibility Criteria

PSE Enrollees March 1978	Number	Percent
TOTAL	742,000	100
Hired under EJPEA project criteria	429,000	58
Title VI projects	347,000	47
Title VI sustainment[a]	82,000	11
Hired under pre-EJPEA criteria	313,000	42
Title II	129,000	17
Title VI sustainment	184,000	25

SOURCE: Computed from data from the Employment and Training Administration, U.S. Department of Labor.

[a] Half of new enrollees for regular Title VI positions.

TABLE 16　Characteristics of Persons Eligible for Title VI Public Service Employment Positions, Before and After the Emergency Jobs Programs Extension Act (percent of total)

Characteristics	Pre-EJPEA Title VI[a]	Post-EJPEA Title VI Projects[b]
TOTAL PERSONS ELIGIBLE	20,228,613	4,430,355
Sex:　Male	56	49
Female	44	51
Age:　16-21	24	20
22-44	51	64
45+	25	16
Race:　White	81	66
Black and other	19	34
Years of education:　0-11	40	54
12	37	33
13+	23	12
Economically disadvantaged	42	93
AFDC recipient	05	48

SOURCE: Computed from March 1976 Current Population Survey, Bureau of the Census; Employment and Training Administration data, U.S. Department of Labor.

[a] Includes persons unemployed 5 weeks or more in calendar 1975 and employed persons with family income below the OMB poverty level.
[b] Persons unemployed 15 weeks or more with family income below 70 percent of the Bureau of Labor Statistics low-income standard in 1975 and persons registered with WIN (fiscal 1976).

TABLE 17 Characteristics of Eligible Population and Participants, by Class of Eligibles, Title VI Projects, Fiscal 1977 (percent of total)

Characteristics	Unemployed 15 Weeks, Low Income Not Receiving AFDC or UI		UI Beneficiaries		AFDC Recipients	
	Eligible Population[a]	New Hires[b]	Eligible Population[a]	New Hires[b]	Registered as Available for Work[c]	New Hires[b]
TOTAL PERSONS	1,353,259	107,751	959,342	24,866	2,117,754	17,895
Sex: Male	65	70	73	78	27	35
Female	35	30	27	22	73	65
Age: 16-21	32	22	8	11	17	18
22-44	52	66	69	68	69	72
45+	17	12	23	22	13	10
Race: White	67	64	84	79	57	49
Black and other	33	36	16	21	43	51
Years of education: 0-11	53	33	44	28	60	38
12	30	35	38	41	33	46
13+	17	31	18	31	7	16
Economically disadvantaged	88	64	86	60	100	100
Proportion of total eligibles and new hires	31	72	22	17	48	12

[a] Current Population Survey, Bureau of the Census, March 1976. (Data are for 1975.)
[b] Continuous Longitudinal Manpower Survey data for April-September 1977, Westat, Inc. Figures for white race include all Hispanics.
[c] WIN data as of June 30, 1976, Employment and Training Administration, U.S. Department of Labor.

members of the eligible population appear to be in financial need; half have received AFDC and 22 percent are UI recipients (Table 17).

Congress also indicated its desire to distribute PSE jobs to those least likely to obtain jobs on their own. While such labor market difficulty cannot be measured directly, it is often correlated with low educational attainment and minority status. The increase in the proportion of nonwhites in the population eligible under EJPEA and the substantial increase in the proportion of persons with less than a high school education are consistent with the congressional desire to shift the orientation of the PSE program toward the unemployed who face structural barriers to employment.

PARTICIPANTS SELECTED FROM THE ELIGIBLE POPULATION

Although EJPEA substantially increased the proportion of disadvantaged persons in the population eligible for nonsustainment Title VI jobs, this increase was not correspondingly reflected in the characteristics of participants hired. Title VI participants hired for projects in fiscal 1977 were significantly less disadvantaged than the eligible population from which they were selected. Indeed, as shown in Chapter 5, the recruitment and hiring processes systematically selected the better qualified, less disadvantaged individuals.

Between April and September 1977, the number of eligible persons was 30 times larger than the number of new hires during the period. While the ratio of eligibles to participants declined as the PSE expansion progressed, there were still 10 eligible persons for each funded position when Title VI employment peaked in March 1978. Thus, local officials were able to exercise considerable discretion in selecting participants. To illustrate: At the peak of the expansion, the eligible population was large enough so that local officials could have filled all of the available project (nonsustainment) Title VI positions with eligible persons with 13 or more years of education. While this of course did not happen, there are significant differences between the characteristics of the eligible population and those of project Title VI participants.

Fifty-four percent of the individuals eligible for projects had not completed high school; only 12 percent had 13 or more years of education (Table 18 and Figure 1). Of those hired in nonsustainment Title VI jobs from April to September 1977, however, only 29 percent had less than a high school education, while 33 percent had at least 13 years of education. Clearly, the better educated came off best in the recruitment and hiring processes.

TABLE 18   Characteristics of Eligible Population and
Participants, Title VI Projects (percent of total)

Characteristics	Persons Eligible for Title VI Projects[a]	Title VI Project Participants[b]
TOTAL PERSONS	4,430,355	145,800
Sex: Male	49	67
Female	51	33
Age: 16-21	20	20
22-44	64	67
45+	16	13
Race: White	66	66
Black and other	34	34
Years of education: 0-11	54	29
12	33	37
13+	12	33
Economically disadvantaged	93	73

SOURCE: March 1976 Current Population Survey, Bureau of the Census; Employment and Training Administration data, U.S. Department of Labor; Continuous Longitudinal Manpower Survey, Westat, Inc.

[a] Persons unemployed 15 weeks or more with family income below 70 percent of the Bureau of Labor Statistics low-income standard budget (1975) and persons registered with WIN (fiscal 1976).
[b] Participant characteristics, Continuous Longitudinal Manpower Survey, April-September 1977. Figures for white race include all Hispanics.

A comparison of other characteristics suggests a similar pattern. Those with the characteristics traditionally associated with success in the labor market fared far better than their more disadvantaged counterparts. Thus, while 93 percent of the eligible population had incomes below the poverty level, 73 percent of nonsustainment Title VI participants had income levels that low. And, although half of the eligible population was female, women constituted only one-third of the participants. Local hiring discretion worked against those groups generally in greatest need of labor market assistance, with the apparent exception of nonwhites. Figure 1 indicates that nonwhites made up 34 percent of both the eligible population and the nonsustainment Title VI participants. But this is not an improvement over their earlier position, since, prior to EJPEA, nonwhites were overrepresent-

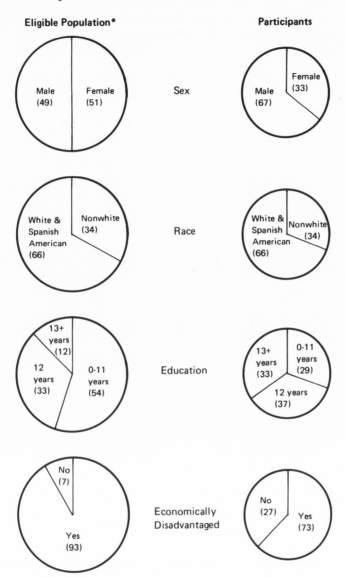

Eligible Population*

Participants

Sex

Male (49) | Female (51)

Male (67) | Female (33)

Race

White & Spanish American (66) | Nonwhite (34)

White & Spanish American (66) | Nonwhite (34)

Education

13+ years (12) | 12 years (33) | 0-11 years (54)

13+ years (33) | 0-11 years (29) | 12 years (37)

Economically Disadvantaged

No (7) | Yes (93)

No (27) | Yes (73)

*1975 data
SOURCE: Current Population Survey, Bureau of Census, Employment and Training Administration, U.S. Department of Labor, and Continuous Longitudinal Manpower Survey, Westat, Inc.

FIGURE 1   Characteristics of Eligible Population and Participants, Title VI Projects, Fiscal 1977

TABLE 19   Public Service Employment Job Referrals and Title VI Project Hires Compared with Eligible Population and Applicant Pools, Fiscal 1977 (percent of total)

Eligibility Categories	Population Eligible for Projects[a]	Employment Service-PSE Applicant Pool	Referrals from Pool to PSE Job Openings	New Title VI Project Hires[b]
ALL CATEGORIES	100	100	100	100
AFDC recipients	48	25	13	12
UI beneficiaries	22	41	26	17
Others unemployed 15 or more weeks with low income	31	34	61	72

SOURCE: Based on March 1976 Current Population Survey, Bureau of the Census; Employment and Training Administration data, U.S. Department of Labor; Continuous Longitudinal Manpower Survey data, Westat, Inc.

[a] 1975 and 1976 data.
[b] Preliminary figures. New hires, April–September 1977, came from other sources as well as the ES-PSE pool.

ed in Title VI jobs in comparison to their proportion in the eligible population.

That the dynamics of the selection process works against those most in need of labor market assistance in several ways becomes clear upon examination of how persons are identified as members of the eligible population, referred to jobs, and hired and by a comparison of the characteristics of potential enrollees at these stages. Table 19 displays the proportion of persons in each eligibility category during four phases of the recruitment and hiring process.

AFDC Recipients

AFDC recipients, for example, are 48 percent of the population eligible for nonsustainment Title VI jobs. But they comprised 25 percent of those registered in the ES–PSE pool and only 12 percent of all nonsustainment Title VI enrollees. It is apparent that outreach efforts were not bringing eligible AFDC recipients into the pool and that AFDC recipients were not referred to jobs in proportion to their representation in the ES–PSE pool.

Several explanations of this selection pattern have been offered: AFDC recipients lacked the skills necessary for the jobs available, sponsors were reluctant to refer predominantly female AFDC recipients to jobs traditionally performed by men, sponsors relied on preselected participants to fill job slots quickly, and such participants are unlikely to be AFDC recipients.

UI Recipients

Another category of persons identified as eligible for Title VI nonsustainment positions was that of unemployment insurance beneficiaries. One-fifth of the eligible population received unemployment insurance. However, UI beneficiaries comprised two-fifths of those referred to the ES–PSE pool. This overrepresentation reflects the fact that the employment service offices, which were largely responsible for the organization of the pools, were in an excellent position to identify and refer UI beneficiaries, since all such persons are registered in their offices. Nonetheless, UI beneficiaries represented only 26 percent of the persons referred from the ES–PSE pool to jobs. Furthermore they accounted for 17 percent of all new hires. While this proportion was much less than their share of the pool, it was more nearly in proportion to their representation in the eligible population than that of the other two target categories.

Other Eligible Persons

The final category of eligibles, "others," consists of persons meeting the income and duration of unemployment requirements, other than AFDC or UI recipients. The experience of persons in the "others" category were markedly different from that of the transfer payment recipients. They accounted for 31 percent of the eligible population and 34 percent of the pool. But their share of referrals to jobs was 61 percent, and, more significantly, they got 72 percent of the new Title VI jobs.

ALLOCATING RESOURCES EQUITABLY

Congress was aware that the eligible population defined by the EJPEA targeting criteria was much larger than could be served at the level of funding contemplated and that hiring agencies were inclined to select the best qualified individuals available. To promote the hiring of disadvantaged participants under these circumstances, Congress required that Title VI nonsustainment jobs be allocated equitably among the categories of eligible persons according to their respective shares in the eligible population. Specifically, the DOL regulations provided that (42 *Federal Register*, p. 55780):

The prime sponsor shall take reasonable steps to ensure that funds . . . are equitably allocated among the categories of eligible persons. . . . Such equitable allocation shall be made in light of the composition of the population of unemployed eligible persons served by the prime sponsor. . . .

The extreme emphasis on speedy implementation, the local recruitment process, the decisions of potential participants, and the proclivity of hiring officials to select the best among those available—all operated to limit the extent to which the various categories of "unemployed eligible persons" were served equitably. This conclusion is supported by a comparison of persons eligible for nonsustainment Title VI and those enrolled in the program in terms of the eligibility categories.

Not only were the allocations of Title VI nonsustainment jobs among the mandated categories different from their proportions in the eligible population, but within each eligible category hiring officials disproportionately selected the better educated, males, and persons with incomes above the poverty level (Table 17).

In the category of "other eligibles," from which the majority of participants were drawn:

- Fifty-three percent of the eligible population had less than a high school education; but of those hired, 33 percent had less than 12 years of school.
- Eighty-eight percent of the eligible population was economically disadvantaged; yet only 64 percent of the participants had incomes below the poverty level.

The same pattern prevailed among the AFDC recipients:

- Sixty percent of the eligible AFDC population had less than a high school education; of those hired, however, only 38 percent had not completed high school.
- Conversely, while 7 percent of the eligible welfare population had 13 or more years of education, 16 percent of the AFDC recipients who were hired had some post-high-school education.

Among UI beneficiaries:

- Forty-four percent of the eligibles had not completed high school; but of those hired, only 28 percent were dropouts.
- Eighty-six percent of the eligible universe was economically disadvan-

taged, compared with 60 percent of the hired persons who were similarly situated.

CHANGES IN PARTICIPANT CHARACTERISTICS

EJPEA had a relatively small effect on the overall characteristics of PSE participants, although there were diverse changes in the characteristics of those in particular programs and a general increase in the proportion of the economically disadvantaged.

• In nonsustainment Title VI (projects), EJPEA has substantially increased the proportion of economically disadvantaged individuals, transfer recipients, and persons likely to be considered structurally unemployed.

• In sustainment Title VI, the characteristics profile of participants reflects the increased emphasis on the economically disadvantaged, but is otherwise not significantly different from their pre-EJPEA counterparts.

• In Title II, EJPEA appears to have accelerated the trend toward serving individuals with fewer traditional labor market disadvantages.

TITLE VI, NONSUSTAINMENT

Despite the selectivity in hiring exercised by prime sponsors, application of the more stringent eligibility requirements of EJPEA substantially altered the characteristics profile of the persons enrolled in Title VI nonsustainment jobs. Those hired under the project criteria in fiscal 1977 were significantly different from fiscal 1976 enrollees and from those now employed in fiscal 1977 sustainment positions. A larger proportion is economically disadvantaged; the percentage that receives transfer payments is up sharply; and the proportion of structurally unemployed persons, whether measured by race, educational attainment, or prior labor force status, has increased substantially.

The proportion of economically disadvantaged participants rose from 43 percent of pre-EJPEA Title VI participants (fiscal 1976) to 83 percent of nonsustainment Title VI participants in fiscal 1977 (Table 20). This was the largest overall change reported in the 22 areas examined in the study. According to the CLMS, there was an increase of 27 rather than 40 percentage points (Appendix C, Table 1).[8]

[8]There are two possible explanations for this discrepancy, both of which suggest that the CLMS figure is more accurate. First, "past experience indicate that some enrollees may give sponsor intake interviewers answers which they feel will facilitate their enrollment, and may give other answers at a later date when their eligibility is no longer at issue" (Westat, Inc.,

TABLE 20   Characteristics of Title VI Participants, Sample Prime Sponsor Areas, Fiscal 1975-1977 (percent of total)

| | | | Fiscal 1977 | |
Characteristics	Fiscal 1975	Fiscal 1976	Sustain- ment[a]	Project
CUMULATIVE ENROLLEES	7,560	20,898	15,564	11,820
Sex: Male	70	65	61	67
Female	30	35	39	33
Age: 16-21	22	21	20	20
22-44	64	65	63	67
45+	14	14	17	13
Race: White	70	68	70	60
Black and other	30	32	30	40
Years of education: 0-11	23	20	19	26
12	43	42	45	45
13+	35	39	36	29
AFDC recipient	9	7	9	17
UI recipient	15	15	17	21
Economically disadvantaged	46	43	56	83
Total veterans	—	—	24	24
Unemployed	89	85	71	93

SOURCE: Prime sponsor records for 22 of the 28 sample areas.
NOTE: Percentages are average of percentages for reporting areas.

[a] Participants enrolled to fill PSE vacancies due to attrition.

It is evident that the proportion of economically disadvantaged persons in the nonsustainment Title VI programs rose substantially following the enactment of EJPEA. The best available evidence suggests that at least 73 percent of the nonsustainment Title VI participants hired from April to September of 1977 was economically disadvantaged.

The congressional objective of moving persons from transfer payment programs into CETA public service employment jobs was, in part, also

1977, p. 5-49). EJPEA, in requiring that participants be low-income individuals, increases the likelihood that the data collected by the prime sponsors will overstate the proportion of economically disadvantaged participants. Second, prime sponsor collected data may overstate the proportion of nonsustainment Title VI participants with income below the level of poverty, because, during the period in question, ETA was preparing to change the definition of economically disadvantaged. Prime sponsors may have begun to include persons with incomes between the poverty level and 70 percent of the BLS lower living standard prior to the end of September 1977 due to some confusion surrounding the change.

achieved. In the 22 sample areas, the proportion of AFDC recipients in projects during fiscal 1977 was 17 percent compared to 7 percent in Title VI programs a year earlier; UI claimants' shares of project positions were 6 percentage points greater than their shares of the pre-EJPEA Title VI positions. The more modest size of this increase may reflect the UI recipients' views of the desirability of PSE jobs and their appraisals of opportunities in the private sector. They are, on the whole, job-ready individuals who may have strong attachments to a particular industry or occupational field. During spells of unemployment, they may prefer to draw UI benefits. The employment service data discussed earlier in this chapter suggests that the lack of referrals was the major cause of nonparticipation among UI claimants. It is likely that this lack of referrals was partly related to the UI claimants' assessments of their alternative income opportunities.

Nonwhites made substantial gains under EJPEA. From fiscal 1976 to fiscal 1977, the proportion of nonwhites in nonsustainment Title VI increased from 32 to 40 percent. There are two possible factors responsible for the change. First, the proportion of nonwhites in the population eligible for projects nationally was significantly greater, 15 percentage points, thus improving their opportunity for selection. Second, PSE jobs may have been more attractive to nonwhites, who had fewer alternative job opportunities than their white counterparts. The CLMS data suggest that, as a group, nonwhite participants had lower incomes, more unemployment, more employability barriers, and more dependents than did white participants.[9]

The educational attainment of participants who were hired under the new EJPEA admission standards was distinctly lower than for persons employed in Title VI jobs before EJPEA. The proportion of participants with less than a high school education rose from 20 to 26 percent, while the proportion with 13 or more years of education declined from 39 percent in fiscal year 1976 to 29 percent a year later.

Changes in the proportion of nonwhites and persons with less than a high school education are especially important in assessing the extent to which the EJPEA targeting criteria reached the structurally unemployed. Of all the groups in the eligible population, these two are likely to experience the greatest difficulty in the labor market. Data collected on persons who terminated from the Title VI program in fiscal 1978 confirms that blacks and persons with 0–11 years of education entered employment at a much lower rate than other groups in the eligible population, such as

[9]Unpublished CLMS data.

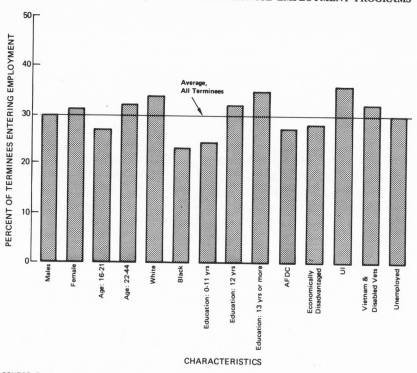

SOURCE: Employment and Training Administration, U.S. Department of Labor

FIGURE 2   Characteristics of Title VI Public Service Employment Terminees Who Entered Employment, Fiscal 1978

UI recipients and veterans (Figure 2). This suggests that the increased participation of nonwhites and persons with less than a high school education in the nonsustainment Title VI program was consistent with the congressional directive to give special consideration to those groups with the fewest prospects for unsubsidized employment.

Prime sponsor records also show that the proportion of participants unemployed prior to entry increased from 85 percent to 93 percent. While there undoubtedly was an increase in the proportion of persons unemployed prior to entry into nonsustainment Title VI jobs, the interpretation of this item is clouded by two developments: (a) the reclassification of participants that took place when participants were transferred between CETA titles[10] and (b) the number of ineligible persons in the program. The

[10]When Title VI funding began to run short in September 1976, Title VI participants were

CLMS indicates that 14 percent of enrollees other than AFDC claimants in nonsustainment Title VI were not unemployed for 15 of the last 20 weeks. These individuals appear to be ineligible. In reviewing participant eligibility, Department of Labor auditors found that failure to meet the unemployment criteria was the leading cause of ineligibility (see Chapter 5). Finally, it should be kept in mind that labor force status as recorded by ETA does not measure the duration of unemployment prior to entry. Consequently, although 93 percent of nonsustainment Title VI participants were unemployed prior to entry, it is not known how many were unemployed 15 of the last 20 weeks.[11]

Prime sponsors did not report on the total proportion of veterans in Title VI prior to EJPEA. The CLMS data indicate that the total proportion of veterans rose from 27 percent in Title VI jobs prior to EJPEA to 31 percent in nonsustainment Title VI jobs in fiscal year 1977 (Appendix C, Table 1). This increase cannot be traced directly to the EJPEA targeting criteria, however. Rather, it is the result of the 35 percent veteran hiring goal that the Department of Labor established at the beginning of the PSE expansion. Although the goal was not reached—the survey data suggest that there was not a sufficient number of available veterans—the proportion of veterans hired did increase significantly.

There can be little doubt, then, that the EJPEA targeting criteria had a significant effect on the characteristics of nonsustainment Title VI participants. There are more economically disadvantaged participants, a larger proportion of transfer recipients, and a greater number of structurally unemployed individuals.

TITLE VI, SUSTAINMENT

As indicated previously, Congress, for political as well as program reasons, did not require that all existing (sustainment) positions under Title VI meet the new eligibility criteria. Indeed, only half of the persons hired after the implementation of EJPEA were required to meet these standards. As a result, the characteristics of sustainment Title VI participants have not changed very much.

transferred into Title II. These participants were moved back into Title VI in February and March 1977 when Title VI funding again became available. These transferees were recorded in "other" labor force status rather than "unemployed." This tended to reduce the proportion of unemployed participants in the pre-EJPEA period.

[11]In fiscal 1976, 52 percent of all PSE enrollees were not unemployed at entry, and 27 percent were unemployed fewer than 14 weeks, according to the Continuous Longitudinal Manpower Survey (Westat, Inc., 1977, p. 6-6, Table 6-2). CLMS data for 1977 show that 35 percent of nonsustainment enrollees were not unemployed and 26 percent more were unemployed less than 14 weeks (Westat, Inc., 1979, Table 19).

In March 1977, when the PSE expansion began, 97 percent of the sustainment Title VI participants were either pre-EJPEA Title VI participants or persons transferred into Title VI from Title II.[12] As the PSE expansion progressed, the proportion of sustainment participants hired under the new eligibility requirements increased.

Since the EJPEA targeting criteria did not affect more than one-third of the sustainment Title VI participants during the period covered by this study, there have been few significant changes recorded in the characteristics profile of sustainment Title VI enrollees. Table 20, which compares the characteristics of enrollees in sustainment Title VI jobs with the characteristics of pre-EJPEA Title VI participants for 22 sample areas, confirms that the EJPEA targeting criteria have not had a major effect on the characteristics (with the exception of family income) of sustainment participants.

Prime sponsor records indicate that the proportion of economically disadvantaged participants increased from 43 percent in the pre-EJPEA period (fiscal 1976) to 56 percent in fiscal 1977.

The proportion of male participants in sustainment programs declined from 65 percent in fiscal 1976 to 61 percent in fiscal 1977. This downturn began in fiscal 1975. The continued decline is attributable to the introduction of projects, with their concentration of male-oriented jobs in nonsustainment Title VI. This concentration was offset by increasing the proportion of jobs filled by women in sustainment Title VI and Title II, where the prime sponsor had more flexibility in creating jobs. (See Chapter 8 for a discussion of the effect of projects on participant characteristics.)

While participants had lower incomes, they do not appear to have been more disadvantaged in terms of their prospects for finding a job. Changes in the other characteristics of sustainment participants—age, race, educational attaiment, and income transfer status—were quite small (Table 20). The effect of EJPEA targeting criteria on the characteristics profile of Title VI sustainment participants was moderated because most were hired under the regular (not project) eligibility criteria. Although the act specified that 50 percent of the replacement hires must meet the same criteria as those for Title VI projects, most sustainment enrollees were either (a) carried on the rolls from before EJPEA or (b) hired with the pre-

---

[12]The EJPEA regulations specifically provided that the eligibility requirements were not to apply to Title II participants transferred into Title VI during the initial separation of Title II and VI participants. This provision enabled prime sponsors to transfer participants hired under the old eligibility requirements into Title VI and fill the positions thus vacated under the less stringent Title II eligibility requirements.

EJPEA criteria. Of the sustainment enrollees in March 1978, when the number peaked, it is estimated that 69 percent were hired with the old criteria.

One would expect, however, to find some changes in the characteristics of newly hired sustainment participants, since half of such participants were required to meet the low-income, long-term unemployed eligibility criteria. In the CLMS data, which permit a comparison between the characteristics of newly hired sustainment participants and those of the pre-EJPEA Title VI participants, some changes do in fact appear. CLMS data show a significant increase in the proportion of economically disadvantaged and AFDC recipients—characteristics related directly to the new eligibility criteria (Appendix C, Table 1). They also show an increase in the proportion of blacks. On the other hand, the proportion of youth and persons with less than a high school education—groups that often experience difficulty in the labor market—declined.

TITLE II

Although EJPEA succeeded in increasing the proportion of disadvantaged participants in the nonsustainment Title VI program, this accomplishment was partially offset by a significant decrease in the proportion of minorities and persons with low educational attainment—groups often associated with structural disadvantage—in Title II. Thus, despite the fact that EJPEA did not change the eligibility requirements for Title II, the impact that it had on the characteristics of Title II participants must be considered.

Table 21 suggests that the participants enrolled in Title II programs following the enactment of EJPEA have fewer structural handicaps than their earlier counterparts. Prior to EJPEA, 32 percent of Title II participants had 13 or more years of education. By the end of the PSE expansion, this proportion had risen to 38 percent. Moreover, the increase came at the expense of those least likely to succeed in the labor market— persons with less than a high school education. Between fiscal years 1976 and 1978 the proportion of high school dropouts in Title II declined 6 percentage points.

Table 21 also shows a 9-point drop in the proportion of nonwhite Title II participants. This is especially material because it occurred during an economic recovery when the proportion of nonwhites in the eligible population was likely to be increasing. A comparison of the ethnic characteristics of Title II and VI participants suggests that nonwhite individuals were more likely to be enrolled in Title VI than in Title II

TABLE 21 Characteristics of Public Service Employment Participants, by Title, Fiscal 1975-1978 (percent of total)

Characteristics	Title II				Title VI				Titles II and VI			
	1975	1976ᵃ	1977	1978	1975	1976ᵃ	1977	1978	1975	1976ᵃ	1977	1978
CUMULATIVE ENROLLEES (thousands)	197	254	348	210	154	493	581	1,008	351	747	929	1,218
Sex: Male	66	64	60	55	70	65	64	62	68	65	63	61
Female	34	36	40	45	30	35	36	38	32	35	37	39
Age: 16-21	24	22	20	21	21	22	20	21	23	22	20	21
22-44	63	64	64	65	65	64	65	65	64	64	65	65
45+	13	14	16	14	14	14	15	14	13	14	15	14
Race: White	65	61	71	70	71	68	66	64	68	66	68	65
Black and otherᵇ	35	39	29	30	29	32	34	36	32	34	32	35
Education: 0-11	28	26	23	20	26	26	27	28	27	26	26	27
(years) 12	42	42	43	42	44	43	42	41	43	43	42	41
13+	30	32	34	38	30	31	31	31	30	31	32	32
AFDC recipient	7	6	6	8	6	6	10	12	7	6	9	11
Economically disadvantagedᶜ	48	47	49	62	44	44	67	81	46	45	60	78
UI recipient	12	13	15	13	15	14	16	15	13	14	16	15
Vietnam veteran	—	4	5	7	—	5	7	8	—	5	6	8
Disabled veteran	—	0	1	1	—	1	1	1	—	1	1	1
Unemployedᵈ	84	77	74	84	88	82	81	90	86	80	78	89

SOURCE: Employment and Training Administration, U.S. Department of Labor.

ᵃ July 1, 1975-June 30, 1976.
ᵇ Includes blacks, American Indians, native Alaskans, Asians, and Pacific Islanders. Also includes Puerto Ricans not classified by ethnic group.
ᶜ Definition changed in fiscal 1978 to include persons with incomes between the Office of Management and Budget poverty level and 70 percent of the Bureau of Labor Statistics lower living standard budget.
ᵈ Proportion of participants unemployed prior to entry declined in fiscal 1976 and 1977 because participants transferred between titles due to funding shortfalls were classified in "other" labor force status rather than by their preentry status.

120

positions. Thus, while nonwhite participation in Title II was declining, the proportion of nonwhites in Title VI rose 5 percentage points. As noted earlier, this increase was concentrated in Title VI projects where the proportion of nonwhites rose 8 percentage points (Table 20).

The reported increase of one-third in the proportion of the economically disadvantaged is at variance with the trends reported in the other socioeconomic characteristics of Title II enrollees. Most of this increase is probably due to the change in the definition of economically disadvantaged that went into effect in October of 1977. The new definition included participants with incomes between the poverty level and 70 percent of the BLS lower-living-standard income level. Adjusting for this change, it is likely that the proportion of economically disadvantaged participants in Title II with income below the poverty level did not increase more than a few percentage points.

The proportion of participants who were unemployed prior to their enrollment in Title II programs has not changed as a result of EJPEA. The apparent increase from fiscal 1976 to 1978 reported in Table 21 is due to the effect of intertitle transfers on the fiscal 1976 and 1977 employment data.

The expansion of Title VI projects under EJPEA created a large number of laboring jobs not suitable for, or unattractive to, women. Concomitantly, jobs typically performed by women were apparently shifted to Title II. The effect of this was to increase by a quarter the proportion of women in Title II.

OVERALL CHANGES IN CLIENTELE

In evaluating the overall effect of EJPEA in terms of its targeting objectives, it is necessary to keep in mind that Congress sought to change the type of persons served only in specific segments of the PSE programs. On this limited basis, the EJPEA targeting criteria were successful. The nonsustainment Title VI program serves a more needy clientele than any previous PSE program. However, it is also clear that by limiting the scope of EJPEA and leaving the requirements for entry into the other PSE programs extremely loose, the aggregate impact of EJPEA was diluted. As a result, Titles II and VI continue to serve a clientele that is predominantly white, male, and well educated.

According to prime sponsor records, the proportion of economically disadvantaged persons participating in Titles II and VI increased from 45 percent in fiscal 1976 to 78 percent in fiscal 1978 (Table 21). However, part of this increase is due to a change in the definition of economically disadvantaged rather than a real change in participant characteristics.[13] In addition, this increase includes a number of ineligible participants who reported lower incomes to the prime sponsor in order to appear eligible. Adjusting for these factors, the actual increase in the proportion of participants with incomes below the level of poverty from fiscal 1976 to fiscal 1978 is approximately 15 percentage points. The relative change in the proportion of Title II and Title VI enrollees who had incomes below the poverty level is confirmed by the CLMS data, which show an increase in the proportion of new PSE participants who were economically disadvantaged from 44 percent in fiscal 1976 to 60 percent in fiscal 1977 (Appendix C, Table 2).

The proportion of participants unemployed prior to entry was reported to have increased from 80 percent in fiscal 1976 to 89 percent in fiscal 1978. However, the proportion of participants unemployed prior to entry was depressed in fiscal 1976 by the classification of intertitle transfers. In fiscal 1975, the proportion of unemployed was 6 percentage points higher than in fiscal 1976 because there were fewer transfers. As a result of the intertitle transfers, it is not possible to estimate accurately the magnitude of the change in the proportion of participants unemployed prior to entry. However, the actual increase is undoubtedly less than 9 percentage points.

The proportion of AFDC recipients rose from 6 percent in fiscal 1976 to 11 percent in fiscal 1978. This, along with the increase in the proportion of economically disadvantaged participants, suggests that the EJPEA targeting criteria have increased the proportion of financially needy individuals served by Titles II and VI. However, while the direction of the change in the proportion of AFDC recipients is consistent with congressional targeting objectives, AFDC recipients are still drastically underrepresented among PSE participants based on their proportion in the eligible population.

That the educational attainment of PSE participants did not change is a particular cause for concern. Thirty-two percent of participants had 13 or more years of education, while 73 percent had at least a high school education. The fact that the level of education did not decrease as a result of these requirements suggests that the income and unemployment criteria of EJPEA were not entirely effective in screening out persons who, in terms of educational background, are not at a disadvantage in the labor market.

---

[13]Beginning in October 1977, the ETA definition of economically disadvantaged was expanded to include persons with incomes between the poverty level and 70 percent of the BLS low income standard. (See U.S. Department of Labor, 1977, p. VII-42.)

The Department of Labor, preoccupied with the task of enrolling sufficient numbers of persons in the expanded PSE programs, did not give adequate attention to who was being enrolled. The relaxed definition of projects, the limited scope of the tightened eligibility requirements, and inadequate eligibility verification requirements all seemed to weaken a strict execution of the targeting objectives.

7 Project Design

Congressional advocates of limited duration projects (Title VI, nonsustainment program) for public service employment anticipated that they would:

- reduce "substitution"—the use of CETA funds for jobs which would be supported from other sources in the absence of CETA;
- provide useful public services; and
- facilitate the phase-down of public service employment when employment opportunities improved.

These expectations were expressed a number of times during the debate on the 1976 revisions of CETA (EJPEA). Congressman Daniels, chairman of the Select Subcommittee on Labor, referred to all three in a House report (U.S. Congress, 1976a, pp. 10–11) submitted with his statement in support of the conference committee report on the amendments to CETA.

. . . because projects have both a defined beginning and a defined end, they make less of an open-ended commitment to continued funding than regular public service employment. Under the bill projects may be for a period no longer than one year and project employees do not have a built-in expectation of continued employment.

. . . critics of public service employment have charged that public service employment jobs are not a net increase to the total stock of jobs. The fact that projects will be sponsored by a variety of groups and governments, none of whom can anticipate the level of funding they will receive, makes it much more difficult for them to reduce their own employment effort in anticipation of funding under the bill.

124

. . . by providing for competition among project applicants the Committee is re-emphasizing its concern and commitment that jobs funded under this legislation continue to be meaningful and productive.

This chapter analyzes aspects of the project program related to the creation of new jobs. While a comparison of the extent of substitution between project and regular public service jobs programs is outside the scope of this study, some of the information incidental thereto is included. CETA legislation has always included a "maintenance of effort" clause that requires assurances that agencies will use PSE funds only to increase employment above the level that otherwise would exist. Nevertheless, studies made before the 1976 revisions of CETA estimate rates of job displacement in the earlier PSE programs, ranging up to 90 percent after 1 year of program operation.[1] Congress viewed this practice as seriously weakening the countercyclical thrust of PSE programs and sought to reduce it by requiring the use of limited duration projects for public service employment in the 1976 amendments of CETA. However, the project requirement applied only to new Title VI positions above the existing "sustainment" level. This had the incidental effect of creating three categories of public service employment programs: Title II, Title VI sustainment, and Title VI projects.

Several aspects of the new project approach distinguished it from other PSE programs and were expected to constrain substitution:

• *Projects were limited to 12 months.* The knowledge that CETA funding would be withdrawn after 12 months was expected to reduce the incentive to use CETA funds for the regular activities of the sponsoring agencies.

• *The emphasis was to be on new or separately identifiable tasks, rather than expansion of ongoing activities.* Adding CETA participants to the regular work force to carry out normal activities was suspected as a prime source of substitution and was to be discouraged.

• *A "substantial portion" of project funding was to be directed to nonproject organizations.* Jobs created by nonprofit organizations were

[1]The National Planning Association estimated displacement at 46 percent (National Planning Association, 1974, p. 47). Alan Fechter estimated displacement at 50 to 90 percent after 1 year (Fechter, 1975). George Johnson and James Tomola found that displacement in the Public Employment Program (PEP) increased from 29 percent after one quarter to 67 percent after 2 years (U.S. Department of Labor, 1975, p. 10). Michael Wiseman reexamined the Johnson and Tomola data and estimated that short-run displacement ranged from 0 to 80 percent, depending on the assumptions used (Wiseman, 1976, p. 86). A study of CETA public service employment made subsequently by the National Academy of Sciences indicated a displacement rate of 35 percent for the first 10 quarters of CETA (National Research Council, 1978b).

presumed to be less likely to substitute for regular government employment.

• *Employment in projects was to be limited to the low-income, long-term unemployed.* Persons in this group are less likely to have the skills needed for employment in regular public service activities.

LIMITED DURATION

The effect on substitution of the 12-month limit on project duration was weakened, because many prime sponsors expected that the requirement would not be rigidly implemented. More than half of the prime sponsors in the study areas surveyed early in 1978 expected to recycle some of their projects. A third thought that the amount of recycling might be as much as 60–80 percent. One respondent put it this way: "Both employing agencies and the CETA staff are assuming that most projects will be renewed with few, if any, changes. If not allowed, there will be severe disruption."

While all project contracts had time limits of 12 months or less, the activities described in most of the 1,100 project summaries that were examined in this study were not the kind usually associated with a limited duration. For example, a 12-month project in a western city was to "provide creative and constructive after-school care for elementary school children of working and single parents."

On the other hand, about a third of all projects were scheduled for less than 12 months, and in about 45 percent of the reporting areas little or no recycling was anticipated. This pattern conforms more closely to the intent of EJPEA.[2]

NEW VERSUS EXPANSION ACTIVITIES

While EJPEA did not prohibit the expansion of regular government activities with CETA resources nor otherwise expressly limit the types of public service alternatives permitted in Title VI projects, the conference report indicated that projects that merely expanded normal ongoing services of government should be minimized.

In the House debate, Congressman Daniels cited the committee report on the House bill (U.S. Congress, 1976a, p. 10), stating:

[2]The 1978 CETA reauthorization act extended the project duration to 18 months and permitted projects which prime sponsors find effective to run for 36 months. These more liberal time limits simplify administration but probably constitute less of a disincentive to substitution than the shorter time limits.

A project is a task that can be defined; it has a beginning and an end. It is different from ordinary public service employment in that it is not an increment to an existing service but rather the accomplishment of a group of persons working independently. The distinction is, of course, not absolute, it is a matter of degree. . . .

The report distinguished between expanding ongoing services and furnishing new ones:

Physical tasks such as planting trees, making bicycle paths, winterizing homes and painting school rooms are fitted to the project concept if performed as separately identifiable tasks, although such tasks might also be performed under regular public service.

The discussion of the final bill in the Senate also discouraged, but did not forbid, the expansion of normal services. Senator Williams stated (*Congressional Record*, 1976, 122(144):p. S16440):

. . . prime sponsors are to be required to maintain services at their normal levels . . . projects may be used only to expand such services or provide services which are not now available. . . .

However, the provision of the bill limiting projects to a 12-month duration strongly suggests that they should be used judiciously and sparingly for increasing the level of customary services. . . .

THE CHANGING DEFINITION OF PROJECTS

Mindful of the concern to create new jobs, the original Department of Labor regulations implementing the project concept defined the types of permissible activities very narrowly. It stated (41 *Federal Register*, p. 46998):

"Project" shall mean a defined task designed to provide a public service. Such tasks shall not expand existing public services, but shall provide a new kind of activity which would cease when the end product representing the accomplishment of a group of persons working independently is complete.

After reviewing objections of prime sponsors that the definition was unnecessarily restrictive, the Department of Labor issued "Implementing Regulations" (42 *Federal Register*, p. 2426), which defined a project as

a definite task, which provides a public service, providing that such service does not expand existing, ongoing services provided by the state, county or municipality. Project funds, for example, could not be used to increase refuse collection from once to twice a week, but could be used to undertake a special cleanup endeavor. . . .

The earlier reference to "a new kind of activity" was omitted.

The legislative provisions and the federal regulations for implementing projects did not become an urgent issue until late January 1977, when the administration's proposed economic stimulus legislation provided for substantial additional Title VI funds for limited-duration projects. This again focused attention on the project definition. Prime sponsors felt that the new definition was still too restrictive and would make it difficult to achieve the enrollment goals in the time stipulated. They pressed for less limiting criteria. Faced with persistent high unemployment and eager for rapid implementation of the large-scale public service employment program, the Labor Department issued a more liberal definition in the revised federal regulations of May 13, 1977, the same day that the president signed the Economic Stimulus Act. Projects were now limited to a definable task or group of related tasks that:

- will be completed within a definable time period, not exceeding 1 year;
- will have a public service objective;
- will result in a specific product or accomplishment;
- would otherwise not be done with existing funds.

In the interest of the speedy implementation of the greatly expanded program, the restraints in the earlier definition aimed at preventing substitution were successively loosened from:

- a new kind of activity that would not expand existing public services and would cease when completed (October 1976); to
- a task that does not expand existing ongoing services (January 1977); to
- a task that would otherwise not be done with existing funds (May 1977).

PRIME SPONSOR RESPONSE TO THE PROJECT CRITERIA

To achieve the countercyclical objectives of the Economic Stimulus Act, the Department of Labor established goals that called for rapid PSE enrollment increases from approximately 300,000 in mid-May 1977 to 725,000 by February 28, 1978.

The administration's enrollment goals were exceeded. By the end of February 1978, about 750,000 persons were working in PSE jobs. The number of Title VI project employees had grown from less than 10,000 at the start of the buildup in May 1977 to 350,000.

CETA officials in 17 of the areas studied stated they would not have been

TABLE 22 Opinions of Local Officials of Revised Title VI Project Criteria, Sample Prime Sponsor Areas (percent of respondents)

Respondent Opinion	CETA Administrators	Other Officials[a]
Revised definition resulted in broader array of activities for project funding	89	89
Revised definition made it easier to meet hiring goals	86	82
Revised definition made it difficult to differentiate between "regular" PSE and project PSE activities	57	54
Number of respondents	(28)	(57)

[a] Primarily chairmen of Manpower Planning Councils and officials of community-based organizations.

able to meet their hiring schedules if the more narrowly defined project criteria of January 1977 had been retained. In 3 other areas they were doubtful, while 8 said the project program could have been implemented under the earlier guidelines. In addition, all but 5 of the 27 areas reporting said that the earlier project definition was not flexible enough to permit the kind of project activities that would be most useful.

Most local CETA officials in the 28 study areas affirmed that the revised project criteria permitted a broader array of activities suitable for project funding and made it easier to meet the hiring goals. However, a majority also said that it was difficult to distinguish project activities from activities carried out under regular (sustainment) PSE programs (Table 22).

Fifty-eight percent of the projects in the sample areas provided new programs and services, 34 percent were expansions of existing programs, and 8 percent were involved in maintaining activities that would have been curtailed in the absence of CETA. Thus, 42 percent were similar to ongoing activities and were more susceptible to substitution than "new" activities. This highlights the trade-off between the objective of constraining substitution by requiring new activities and the ease of implementation and local flexibility. However, the early emphasis on new activities was a factor in reducing the extent of substitution.

In reauthorizing CETA in 1978, Congress chose to avoid explicit restrictions on the types of activities permissible in Title VI projects. The definition of projects in the reauthorization act is the same as in the May 13, 1977, regulations except that the 12-month limit on project duration was changed to 18 months.

EXPANDING PARTICIPATION IN PSE PROJECTS

The Congress believed that a wide distribution of project funds would have salutary effects both in creating new positions and in generating useful projects. To encourage project operation by a broad spectrum of local organizations, Congress defined "project applicants" to include state and local government agencies, school systems, organizations serving Indians or Hawaiians, community-based organizations, and other nonprofit organizations.[3] The conference committee report on the 1976 amendments stated (U.S. Congress, 1976b, p. 17):

The Conferees expect prime sponsors to provide a substantial portion of the project funds to nonprofit agencies which both insure that real new jobs are created and avoid the substitution of federal funds for services customarily provided by state and local governments.

The use of nonprofit organizations to employ project participants was assumed to reduce the likelihood of substitution, since their activities are unlikely to replace regular governmental services. The views of local officials support this premise. Only 4 percent of the officials thought that relieving the fiscal problems of local government by taking over functions normally provided by government agencies was an important effect of projects operated by nonprofit organizations, while the proportion who saw it as an important outcome of government agency projects and of sustainment PSE was 29 and 38 percent, respectively. The possible maintenance of effort problem within the private nonprofit organizations was not adressed by Congress.

The goal of distributing project funds to a broader group of project applicants was generally achieved. Governmental agencies in the 23 areas that supplied data on the question received 69 percent of the project funds; nonprofit organizations received the remaining 31 percent. Agencies participating in CETA for the first time obtained 14 percent of the project funds. At the end of fiscal 1977, the proportion of all persons in PSE jobs sponsored by nonprofit organizations was substantially larger in Title VI projects (30 percent) than in either Title VI sustainment (19 percent) or in Title II (15 percent).

ELIGIBILITY CRITERIA

As noted earlier, the 1976 revision of CETA was intended to assure that persons who had experienced the greatest difficulty in obtaining employ-

[3]Section 701(a)(15) of CETA as amended October 1, 1976.

TABLE 23   Selected Characteristics of New Enrollees in Title VI Projects, Title VI Sustainment, and Title II, Fiscal 1977 (percent of new enrollees)

	Title VI		
Characteristics	Projects	Sustainment	Title II
Eleven or less school grades completed	29	21	22
Female	33	37	39
Nonwhite and Hispanic[a]	41	35	32
42-44 years of age	67	68	63
AFDC recipient	15	8	4
Economically disadvantaged	73	57	46
Employment barrier[b]	28	21	25

SOURCE: Continuous Longitudinal Manpower Survey, Westat, Inc.

[a] Nonwhite includes black and other races.
[b] Includes health problem, criminal record, limited English, and other job-related difficulties.

ment were served more fully in public service employment programs. Moreover, serving those most in need was also expected to help control substitution. The Congressional Budget Office concluded that fiscal substitution would be less likely in EJPEA programs than in previous PSE programs because "The enrollees are less likely to have the skill characteristics of those who would normally be hired" and "Local projects are not likely to produce goods and services normally produced by state and local governments."[4]

The more restrictive eligibility criteria for project jobs had a decided effect on the size and the characteristics of the population eligible for PSE jobs and resulted in project participants who generally were more disadvantaged in the job market than those hired for Title II or VI sustainment PSE. Higher proportions of project employees had less than a high school education, were nonwhite, came from families receiving AFDC, were economically disadvantaged, and suffered from employment barriers such as a health problem, criminal record, or limited English speaking ability (Table 23).

The characteristics and skills of the eligible participants were a significant factor in decisions on the kinds of project activities to undertake, especially those operated by government agencies. Restricting eligibility to the low-income, long-term unemployed resulted in an

[4]*Congressional Record*, August 10, 1976, p. S14076.

TABLE 24 Employment in State and Local Governments Compared with Title VI Project and Sustainment Public Service Employment, by Occupational Group, 1977 (percent of total)

Occupational Group	All State and Local Government	Title II PSE	Title VI Sustainment	Title VI Projects Total	Title VI Projects Government Agencies
ALL OCCUPATIONS	100	100	100	100	100
Total white-collar	65	51	46	36	31
Professional, technical, and administrative	45	23	20	19	14
Clerical	19	28	25	17	17
Total blue-collar	13	29	35	47	58
Craftsmen	5	8	9	13	17
Operatives	4	6	5	5	2
Non-farm laborers	4	14	21	29	39
Service workers	22	20	19	17	10

SOURCE: Compiled from unpublished 1977 Current Population Survey data, Bureau of the Census; unpublished Continuous Longitudinal Manpower Survey data, Westat, Inc.; and project data summaries for the 28 study areas.
NOTE: Details may not add to totals because of rounding.

emphasis on public works and parks projects, generally for outdoor cleanup and landscaping, which called primarily for unskilled workers. The occupations of project employees, especially those in government-sponsored projects, are sharply different from the occupational pattern of regular government employment and reveal a greater shift from the regular pattern of government employment than do Title II and VI sustainment PSE. Projects require relatively fewer professional and technical workers, a higher proportion of blue-collar workers (especially laborers), and relatively fewer service workers (Table 24 and Figure 3).

The heavier concentration in the lower skill categories and an occupational pattern markedly dissimilar from the employment matrix of the regular public sector suggest that substitution was less likely to occur in PSE projects.

WAGE RATES

Prior to the 1978 CETA reauthorization, wages for PSE jobs paid from CETA funds were limited to an average of no more than $7,800 for the country as a whole and $10,000 for any position. However, there was no limit on the extent to which CETA wages could be supplemented with local funds and some jobs were reported to pay $15,000 to $20,000 a year. Supplementation of maximum levels was sometimes necessary, particularly in high-wage areas, since employing agencies were required to pay CETA workers the prevailing wage.

Limiting the level of wages for PSE jobs was expected to discourage substitution because it was assumed that well-qualified persons sought for regular public sector activities would not be attracted by the lowered CETA wage levels. However, as has been noted, high rates of substitution were reported for sustainment PSE although the wage provisions for project and sustainment PSE were the same. Indeed, average beginning wages for PSE jobs were nearly the same—$3.49 per hour for Title II, $3.56 per hour for Title VI projects, and $3.58 per hour for Title VI sustainment.[5]

Wage rates and the effects of the new wage provisions in the CETA reauthorization are discussed more fully in Chapter 9.

THE RESTRAINING INFLUENCE OF PROJECTS

The study data indicate that, in the first year of operation, PSE projects were much less likely than sustainment PSE to result in the substitution of

---

[5]Unpublished data, Continuous Longitudinal Manpower Survey, Westat, Inc.

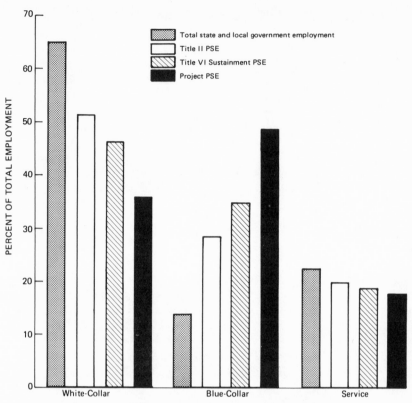

SOURCE: Current Population Survey, Bureau of the Census, and Continuous Longitudinal Manpower Survey, Westat, Inc.

FIGURE 3   Total State and Local Government and CETA Public Service Employment, by White-Collar, Blue-Collar, and Service Occupations, 1977

CETA funds to pay for jobs that would otherwise have been supported from other sources. In 15 of the 25 areas, field observers reported that practically none of the Title VI project activities would have been supported with local funds because local revenues were inadequate. These comments were typical:

The city is in a tight financial situation. . . . most of the PSE work would simply not have been undertaken if CETA funds had not been available. Probably no local funds would be made available.

The projects are important public services but the political climate throughout the county is for tax relief rather than service expansion. It is doubtful that the jobs would have been created without CETA.

Field observers in nine other areas said that a small share of project activities would have been provided in the absence of CETA. In one area it appeared that substitution was more extensive.

Local officials, when asked about specific projects in their communities, reported overwhelmingly that they would not have been financed in the absence of CETA. When asked in another query to rate project and sustainment PSE in terms of job creation, two-thirds replied that projects were more likely to result in net job creation. A study of substitution under the Emergency Jobs Programs Extension Act, made by the Brookings Institution, also found that the rate of substitution in projects was only half as high as that of regular public service employment (National Commission for Employment Policy, 1979, p. 18).

SUMMARY AND CONCLUSIONS

EJPEA's 12-month limit on the duration of individual projects was only partially effective in discouraging substitution. More than half of the reporting areas discounted the 12-month limit and expected to "recycle" some of their projects.

Initially, the Department of Labor sought to strengthen the effectiveness of projects in controlling substitution by restricting projects to "new kinds of activities." Pressures arising from the administration's emphasis on sharply expanded and rapid hiring for economic stimulus purposes led the department to abandon this limitation and to permit program administrators to use projects for the expansion of regular government activities, thus increasing the likelihood of substitution. More than 40 percent of the projects were found to be either expansion or maintenance of ongoing activities.

Greater use of nonprofit organizations for project PSE was a positive factor in controlling substitution, as were the more restrictive criteria for project participants. On balance, the project design for employing jobless persons, although compromised for the sake of speedy implementation, served the intended purpose of creating new jobs and useful services with less potential for substitution than in sustainment PSE programs.

Measures to restrain substitution are not without their costs. The price may be less useful services, less enrollment of the most needy, and less transition of project participants into nonsubsidized jobs. The most useful community services are often those that expand regular activities of government and nonprofit organizations. If emphasis is placed on new types of services to reduce the possibility of substitution, it is likely to be at the expense of usefulness.

Using nonprofit organizations to operate projects may be effective in controlling substitution. However, these institutions tend to employ the most qualified of the persons eligible, and this conflicts with the objective of employing those who are most in need.

Both of these strategies, PSE jobs in new activities and the use of nonprofit organizations, are less likely to result in the transfer of CETA employees into regular jobs. Conversely, PSE employment in an ongoing activity of a government agency increases the possibility that the PSE worker may be absorbed by the agency operating the project. Here again, the objective of constraining substitution by these devices collides with the job placement objective of CETA.

8 Project Services

When Congress mandated the use of projects for the expansion of CETA public service employment, it wanted to be sure that these projects would furnish useful public services. Carl Perkins, the Chairman of the House Committee on Education and Labor, expressed this interest during the debate on the 1976 legislation [*Congressional Record*, 1976, 122(141):H10400]:

> . . . we have occasionally had a hard time identifying the specific accomplishments of public service employment beyond the primary one of providing an unemployed person with a job. . . . By moving in the direction of projects which will perform some new or different service, we should add a lot more visibility to the use of this money so that people can actually see what their tax dollars are doing for them.

This chapter presents judgments of project usefulness by field researchers and local officials and an analysis of project activities. It describes typical project activities and occupations in each major public service area and indicates how projects are affected by the qualifications of the available applicants. The services and occupations in government agency and nonprofit organization projects are compared and project occupations are matched against those of the long-term unemployed.

137

PERCEPTIONS OF PROJECT USEFULNESS

When local officials were asked about project services, 95 percent of the responses rated them as "very useful." Half of the replies came from CETA administrators, and most of the rest were from members of CETA planning councils.

Their views were supported, but less overwhelmingly, by the field research associates. In about two-thirds of the prime sponsor areas, the research associates reported that make-work was insignificant or represented only a small portion of total project effort. In the remaining areas, make-work was estimated at 10 to 25 percent of the total project activities, and in a few instances it was described as substantial.

Activities identified as make-work included the cleaning of roadsides and ditches, arts projects, and surveys of community needs. However, perceptions of make-work lie in the eyes of the beholder. Arts projects and roadside cleaning considered as make-work by some would be viewed by others as useful for improving the quality of life in their community.[1] Some of the marginal outdoor cleanup and beautification projects were attributed to pressures from the Department of Labor for rapid hiring. They were undertaken because they could be implemented speedily.

The conclusion that most project activities were useful was consistent with results of other studies of public service employment. A recent report on Title VI project activities of 30 areas states (MDC, Inc., 1978, p. 23):

Researchers were convinced that most sponsors generated proposals that local officials perceived as both useful and needed. The projects . . . clearly amounted to more than leaf-raking.

A Brookings Institution study (National Commission for Manpower Policy, 1978a, p. 96), referring to all CETA public service employment, including project activities, reported that "Little evidence was found by associates that PSE is a make-work and leaf-raking program."

PRIORITY RATING OF SERVICES

Funding priorities reflect judgments of service usefulness in relation to costs. Resources are limited; demand for services are not and a choice must be made. How high on local priority lists are Title VI activities? When asked whether specific Title VI projects would be funded with local resources if local revenues were 25 percent greater than at present, local

[1] A national survey of opinions on unemployment and related problems found that "cleaning up neighborhoods" ranked as the second most useful activity for persons in jobs created by the federal government to attack the unemployment problem (Public Research, 1978, p. 114).

TABLE 25   Percent of Title VI Projects Likely to be Financed with Local Funds if Local Revenues Were 25 Percent Greater, by Area Unemployment Level, Sample Prime Sponsor Areas

Type of Project	All Sample Areas	High Unemployment Areas	Low Unemployment Areas
Government and nonprofit organization projects	34	37	26
Government projects	37	39	33
Nonprofit organization projects	31	36	19

SOURCE: Based on responses of local officials with respect to 110 projects.

officials in the 28 study areas said one-third of the projects would probably be supported, but two-thirds would not (Table 25).

Project usefulness was limited by some of the CETA provisions. The PSE titles seek to create additional jobs and therefore prohibit the funding of activities that would be supported from other sources in the absence of CETA. Consequently, project activities tend to be lower in priority than those currently supported by local tax revenues. In the interest of maximizing the number of jobs, at least 85 percent of PSE funds had to be used for participant wages and fringe benefits. This discouraged the development of desirable projects that required larger expenditures for materials and administration. To serve persons most in need of jobs, projects could hire only the low-income, long-term unemployed—many of whom were relatively unskilled. The need to design projects for these persons (discussed below) sometimes limited their usefulness. Finally, pressure for large-scale and rapid implementation was a significant factor in the choice of some lower priority activities.

The expectation that project activities, especially those of nonprofit organizations, would be supported if greater local revenues were available was reported more frequently in areas of high unemployment. The demand for public services in such areas was apparently not as well satisfied through their regular budgets as in areas of low unemployment. A higher priority was also somewhat more likely for government than for nonprofit organization projects.

PERFORMANCE OF PROJECT WORKERS

How project workers do their jobs has attracted as much attention as what they are doing. Looking at job performance, local officials rated project participants as "about the same as non-CETA workers doing similar work" in 71 percent of the responses. The remaining answers were divided almost equally between those who considered project workers to be above average and those who rated them below par.[2] Poor performance was attributed to high turnover in a few cases and to poor motivation because of the short-term nature of the jobs in other instances.

PARTICIPANT QUALIFICATIONS AND PROJECT DESIGN

The qualifications of persons eligible for jobs were a significant factor in the design of Title VI projects, especially those operated by government agencies. In the 1976 revisions to Title VI, Congress sought to ensure that public service employment programs would be directed more than previously to persons who faced the most difficulty in obtaining work. This group includes many who, because of inadequate education, lack of experience, minority status, or other disadvantage, find it especially difficult to obtain employment.

Local officials reported that the skills available among persons eligible for employment influenced the design of Title VI projects in 24 of the 28 areas. In 15 of the areas, CETA staff anticipated that a high proportion of the eligible persons would have few skills, and they advised agencies that might sponsor projects to design activities for this group. In the other nine areas, project delays were encountered because the skills necessary were unavailable or had been exhausted from the pool of eligibles. Some of those projects ultimately found persons with the necessary skills. In other cases the projects were redesigned or dropped. In the four remaining areas, the tighter eligibility requirements posed no problem. High unemployment ensured an adequate supply of persons even for projects needing a wide range of skills.

Jobs for unskilled workers were created mainly through government agency projects and resulted in an emphasis on parks and public works projects. Almost 30 percent of project employment was in such activities, i.e., developing parks and recreation facilities, maintaining grounds, cleaning streets, collecting garbage, flood control, and repairing streets and sewers. Field researchers for a few areas found that creating projects to match the skills of the eligible participants resulted in some activities of little value.

---

[2]The study of public service employment by the Brookings Institution also reported that PSE participants (including projects and regular PSE) performed about as well as other employees (National Commission for Employment Policy, 1978a, p. 62.)

SERVICES AND AKILLS

Title VI projects span a broad spectrum of local government and nonprofit organization activities—from cleaning ditches to urban planning, from tutoring slow learners to paintings and sculpture for public buildings, and from developing parks and playgrounds to the weatherization of homes of the poor.[3] Occupations ranged from laborer to engineer, from construction craftsman to social worker, and from office clerk to teacher.

The largest share of project employment was in public works, which accounted for 76,000 positions or 23 percent of the total. The activities were mainly maintenance and repair of public areas and facilities, not new construction. Social services, education, and parks and recreation each accounted for over 55,000 positions or 18 percent of the total. Of the remaining activities—housing, health and hospitals, law enforcement, general administration, creative arts, and "other"—none employed more than 7 percent of the total (Table 26).

Almost half of all project positions were in occupational groups with relatively high skills, including craftsmen, professional, technical and administrative workers, and paraprofessionals. However, the single occupation with the largest share of project employment was also the least skilled. Laboring positions accounted for 28 percent of all project jobs. The remaining jobs were filled by clerical workers, service workers, and operatives (Table 26).

Public Works

All PSE projects for public works use high proportions of blue-collar workers—89 percent overall. However, projects for building and equipment maintenance and repair use a much higher proportion of skilled blue-collar worker than other public works projects. Forty-five percent of the jobs were for craftsmen and only 26 percent for laborers. Prime sponsors reported the use of construction workers to build shelving, painters to work on county-owned buildings, maintenance mechanics to renovate air-conditioning systems, and laborers to clean and repaint fire hydrants. In

---

[3]A sample of about 1,100 Project Data Summaries (PDSs) representing the Title VI project activities of the 28 areas in the study were examined to develop information on the characteristics of PSE projects. The PDSs were the basis for estimating employment by activity and occupation in government and nonprofit organization projects, high and low unemployment areas in the city, county, and balance-of-state areas. Information on wages and the size of projects was also developed from the PDS sample. The sample is described in Appendix A.

TABLE 26 Title VI Project Employment, by Public Service Function and by Occupational Group, 1977 (percent of total)

Public Service Function	Number	Percent of Total	Occupational Groups							
			All Occupations	Professional, Technical, and Administrative	Paraprofessional[a]	Clerical	Craft Workers	Operatives	Laborers	Service Workers
TOTAL	326,000	100	100	14	17	12	17	3	28	8
Public works and conservation	76,000	23	100	3	b	5	22	5	62	2
Building and equipment maintenance and repair	13,000	4	100	1	1	1	45	14	26	12
Other public works	63,000	19	100	3	—	6	17	3	70	1
Social services	59,000	18	100	26	36	16	4	4	1	14
Education	57,000	18	100	14	31	19	15	1	13	7
Teaching related	24,000	7	100	20	58	8	2	b	7	3
Buildings and grounds	14,000	4	100	—	3	7	46	1	35	8
Other services	19,000	6	100	17	14	41	8	2	5	12
Parks and recreation	56,000	17	100	8	8	2	19	3	58	2
Facilities	42,000	13	100	1	—	1	23	2	72	b
Services	13,000	4	100	32	34	4	4	4	13	8
Housing	24,000	7	100	6	5	9	62	5	11	1
Health and hospitals	17,000	5	100	17	32	16	5	4	5	21
Law enforcement	14,000	4	100	17	7	23	1	1	b	50
General administration	8,000	2	100	30	3	66	—	—	1	—
Creative arts	7,000	2	100	75	16	6	2	1	—	—
Other	9,000	3	100	26	14	25	15	1	11	8

SOURCE: Expanded U.S. totals based on sample of Project Data Summaries for 28 study areas.

NOTE: Detail may not add to total because of rounding.

[a] Positions in which the workers perform some of the duties of a professional person or technician, but which do not require the formal training or experience normally required of a professional or technician.

[b] Less than 0.5 percent.

TABLE 27   Title VI Project Employment in Public
Works, by Subactivity, 1977 (percent of total)

Subactivity	Percent
ALL PUBLIC WORKS	100
Grounds maintenance and beautification	25
Buildings and equipment maintenance and repair	17
Street, sidewalk, and sewer repair	14
Street and alley cleaning	10
Flood and erosion control, drainage, and water area cleanup	8
Environment and conservation	6
Garbage collection	5
Other public works	14

SOURCE: Expanded to U.S. total based on sample of Project Data Summaries for 28 study areas.

other public works activities, projects employed primarily unskilled labor, an average of 70 percent of total employment.

The percentage distribution of project employment in public works by major subactivities is shown in Table 27.[4]

Social Services

Title VI projects included a variety of social services with no strong concentration in one field. Among the services most frequently provided are:

• support for former mental patients in making an adjustment to "outside" living;
• day care, recreation, and low-cost meals for the elderly;
• shelters and counseling for battered women and their children;
• surveys of community needs for social services and the availability of such services;
• job search assistance to veterans, youth, and the elderly;
• treatment for alcoholics;
• expansion of legal aid and social services; and
• home management training for tenants of housing projects.

[4]Projects that included more than one type of activity were classified by the activity with the largest share of project positions.

Skills employed in the social service projects were heavily white collar—78 percent of total. Paraprofessionals were the largest occupational group; they advised the elderly, minorities, and economically disadvantaged persons on services available, acted as parolee service aides, handled community relations in housing projects, assisted adoption agencies, worked with students with poor school attendance, and conducted surveys. Social workers made up more than half of the next largest occupational group in the social services function—the professional and technical workers.

Education Services

Only 42 percent of the project activities in education was related directly to instruction. Instruction-related projects included a high proportion of teacher assistants, who were classified as paraprofessionals (Table 26). They were tutors for immigrants and underachievers, aides for students with visual or other learning handicaps, and assistants for pilot reading programs.

About one-fourth of the workers in education services projects were occupied with maintaining school buildings and grounds and almost half of them were craftsmen. Relatively high proportions of general maintenance workers and painters were used. Smaller numbers of skilled workmen such as carpenters, plumbers, masons, and equipment repairmen were employed. All these workers were classified as craftsmen, although a few were reported as trainees. Activities under education classified as "other services" included efforts to reduce truancy, cafeteria operations, and office services.

Parks and Recreation

The development and maintenance of facilities took about three-fourths of total park and recreation PSE employment; recreation services, the remainder. Many projects for the development and maintenance of park facilities require the same skills as those for public works outdoor maintenance and beautification. A high proportion of the project jobs (72 percent) were thus for unskilled labor. However, recreation services call for different qualifications. These projects employed skilled personnel to teach water safety to school children, supervise arts, crafts, and sports programs, expand day camp activities, and promote Boys and Girls Clubs.

Housing

Housing activities, which employed 7 percent of all project workers, were devoted primarily to weatherization and repair of homes of low-income families. These projects were also supported for their energy conservation features. The home insulation program was often sponsored by community based organizations, which link funds from the Community Services Administration for insulation materials with labor paid by CETA. There were also a few projects for improving the maintenance and security of public housing.

Health and Hospitals

Health services included screening persons for hypertension, providing emergency services, and supplementing the nurses' aides and ward clerk staffs.

Law Enforcement

Law enforcement, corrections, and court-related activities depend heavily on service workers, and half the employees in these projects, including police officers, police aides, correctional officers, and security guards for public buildings, were classified in this category. In Chester County, Pennsylvania, an innovative project employed police officers, community relations specialists, and outreach workers of all races to improve relations between police and ethnic communities.

The Arts

Creative arts projects, which accounted for only 2 percent of all project employment, had the highest proportion of professional and technical workers—75 percent. Musicians performing at hospitals, convalescent homes, and schools; dance instructors organizing programs for students, senior citizens, and the handicapped; and artists working to establish a neighborhood arts program were typical activities.

GOVERNMENT AND NONGOVERNMENT PROJECTS

The role of nonprofit organizations was significantly larger as a result of EJPEA than it had been before. By the end of 1977, 30 percent of all project enrollees were in activities sponsored by nonprofit organizations compared to 15 percent in PSE programs in 1975.

The Conference Committee on the Emergency Jobs Programs Extension Act had encouraged the use of nonprofit organizations to operate Title VI projects on the premise that projects of nonprofit organizations were less likely to result in substitution and would increase the likelihood that "project jobs would be meaningful and productive."

Among nonprofit organizations, about 30 percent of employment was in projects sponsored by community-based organizations, and the rest was in projects conducted by various local social service agencies.

Government projects were concentrated in public works and the development of parks and recreation facilities, which together accounted for 54 percent of employment (Table 28 and Figure 4). Almost three out of five of the jobs in the government projects were characterized as blue-collar, traditionally male positions and almost 40 percent were in the laborer category (Table 29 and Figure 5). The project activities of the nonprofit organizations, on the other hand, were largely in social services, improving the housing of low-income families, and special instruction for students with learning difficulties. Seven percent of nonprofit project employment was in creative arts activities. Nonprofit groups devoted a larger share of their project to health and hospitals than did government agencies. Social services, teaching, arts, and health activities employed chiefly professional and paraprofessional workers, often women. Housing improvement projects required blue-collar workers, primarily craftsmen. Thus, 70 percent of nonprofit project jobs were in three high-skill groups: professional and technical workers, paraprofessionals, and craftsmen.

The occupational composition of projects operated by government agencies is very similar to that of the long-term unemployed population, but not necessarily similar to the low-income long-term unemployed from whom project enrollees are drawn. Government projects used about the same proportion of professional, technical and managerial, and clerical workers as were found among the long-term unemployed in 1977. The projects used a somewhat higher proportion of blue-collar workers but these were primarily in the laborer group (Table 30).

While the relatively high proportion of laboring jobs in the government agency projects indicates the degree to which these agencies were creating activities to employ persons with minimum skills and the ease with which projects employing such workers could be launched, the concentration on laboring jobs traditionally filled by men constrained the number of jobs for women, who constituted 51 percent of the eligible group, but only 33 percent of project employment.

Nonprofit organizations tended to use projects to promote the same kinds of social services they normally furnish. As a consequence, the proportions of professional, technical, and managerial workers are much

TABLE 28   Title VI Project Employment, by Function and by Type of Project Sponsor, 1977 (percent of total)

Functional Area	Total	Type of Project Sponsor	
		Government Agency	Nonprofit Organizations
ALL FUNCTIONAL AREAS	100	100	100
Education	18	19	13
Teaching related	7	6	10
Buildings and grounds	4	6	1
Other services	6	7	2
Social services	18	8	40
Health and hospitals	5	3	8
Parks and recreation	17	21	9
Facilities	13	17	5
Services	4	4	4
Creative arts	2	*a*	7
Public works	23	33	3
Grounds maintenance and beautification	6	8	1
Building and equipment maintenance	4	6	*a*
Street and sewer repair	3	5	—
Street cleaning	2	3	*a*
Drainage and flood control	2	3	*a*
Garbage collection	1	2	—
Environment and conservation	1	1	2
Other public works	3	5	*a*
Housing	7	4	15
Law enforcement	4	5	2
General administration	2	3	—
Other	3	2	3
Total employment	(326,000)	(227,000)	(99,000)

SOURCE: Expanded to U.S. total based on sample of Project Data Summaries for the 28 study areas.
NOTE: Detail may not add to total because of rounding.

a Less than 0.5 percent.

TABLE 29   Title VI Project Employment, by Occupational Group and by Type of Project Sponsor, 1977 (percent of total)

Occupational Group	Total	Government Agency	Nonprofit Organizations
ALL OCCUPATIONAL GROUPS	100	100	100
Total white collar	43	35	62
Professionals, technical, and managerial	14	10	25
Social workers	4	2	8
Teachers	2	2	3
Writers, artists, entertainers	2	1	5
Other professional/technical and administrative	7	5	9
Paraprofessionals[a]	17	12	26
Social work paraprofessionals	7	5	12
Other paraprofessionals	10	7	14
Clerical workers	12	13	11
Typists, secretaries, and stenographers	4	4	5
Other clerical workers	9	9	6
Total blue collar	48	58	27
Craftsmen	17	17	19
Building and equipment maintenance and repair	10	10	12
Weatherization craftsmen	2	b	5
Other craftsmen	5	7	1
Operatives	3	3	4
Laborers	28	39	5
Grounds and streets cleanup and maintenance workers	22	30	4
Other laborers	6	8	1
Total service workers	8	8	11
Protective service workers	3	3	3
Other service workers	5	5	7

SOURCE: Expanded to U.S. total based on sample of Project Data Summaries for the 28 study areas.
NOTE: Detail may not add to total because of rounding.

[a] Positions in which the workers perform some of the duties of a professional person or technician, but which do not require the formal training or experience normally required of a professional or technician.
[b] Less than 0.5 percent.

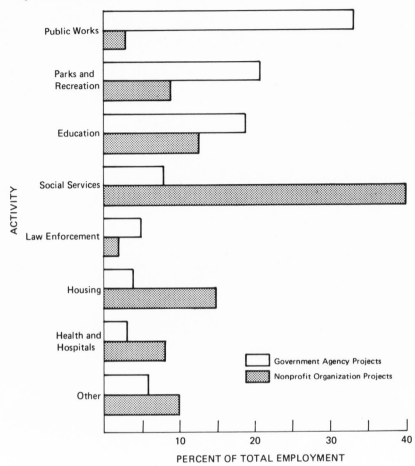

SOURCE: Project Data Summaries

FIGURE 4   Title VI Project Employment in Government and in Nonprofit Organizations, by Type of Activity, 1977

higher than are found among the long-term unemployed. Because of their emphasis on social services, teaching, and health activities, the nonprofit projects were a better source of jobs for women than were the government projects.

In broad terms the projects of government agencies created jobs for men with few skills, while the projects of nonprofit organizations focused more on the services to be provided and less on meeting the job needs of persons with few skills. Although data are not available on proportions of men and

TABLE 30   Title VI Project Employment, by Occupational Group and by Type of Project Sponsor, Compared with Long-Term Unemployed, 1977 (percent of total)

Occupational Group	Long-Term Unem-ployed	Type of Project Sponsor		
		Total	Govern-ment Agencies	Nonprofit Organi-zations
ALL OCCUPATIONAL GROUPS[a]	100	100	100	100
Total white collar	33	37	31	49
Professionals, technical, and managerial	13	21	15	34
Clerical workers	15	16	15	15
Sales workers	5	—	—	—
Total blue collar	43	48	58	27
Craftsmen	12	17	17	19
Operatives	21	3	3	4
Laborers	10	28	39	5
Service workers	14	15	11	24
No previous work experience	10	—	—	—

SOURCE: 1977 employment and earnings data, Bureau of Labor Statistics, U.S. Department of Labor; PSE project employment expanded to U.S. total based on sample of Project Data Summaries for the 28 study areas.

[a] In this table the paraprofessionals, shown as a separate group in previous tables, have been classified in the professional, clerical, and service worker groups to conform with the Census-CPS system used for the long-term unemployed.

women in government and nonprofit projects, it appears clear from the activities and occupations that women made up a much higher proportion of employment in the projects of nonprofit organizations.

IMPACT OF PROJECTS ON GOVERNMENT SERVICES

PSE projects had only a minor effect on total government employment. In three functional areas, however, the impact was significant. The 48,000 project jobs in parks and recreation services made up 30 percent of government employment in the function, and PSE workers in government projects for public works and social services were 6 percent and 4 percent, respectively, of total employment in those functions (Table 31).

The concentration of government projects on parks and public works

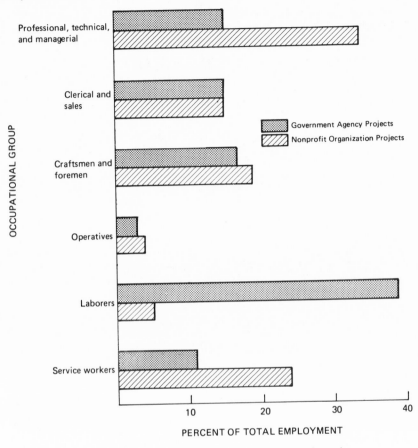

FIGURE 5 Title VI Project Employment in Government and in Nonprofit
Organizations, by Occupational Group, 1977

has been attributed to an emphasis on developing jobs for blue-collar
workers with few skills and the ability to start such activities quickly.
Social services, however, require mainly professional and paraprofessional
workers, as well as some clerical and service workers, and concentration
on this activity probably reflected an interest among government agencies
in meeting the social service needs as well as the employment needs of the
low-income population.

TABLE 31   Employment in Title VI Government
Agency Projects as Percent of Total State and Local
Government Employment, by Function, 1977

Functional Area	PSE Projects as Percent of Total
TOTAL	2
Parks and recreation	30
Public works	6
Social services	4
Law enforcement and corrections	1
General administration	1
Education	1
Health and hospitals	1
Other	2

SOURCE: Computed from Project Data Summaries for 28 study areas
(expanded to U.S. totals) and Public Employment in 1977, Bureau of
the Census.

PROJECT SERVICES IN CITIES AND BALANCE-OF-STATE AREAS

The kinds of activities and occupations found in Title VI projects varied in
some respects with the type of prime sponsor jurisdiction—city, county,
consortium, or balance of state.[5] The sharpest differences were between the
most and the least densely populated areas. Characteristically, cities placed
greater emphasis on social services and law enforcement, while balance-of-
state areas concentrated more on public works, school facility maintenance, and conservation (Table 32).

These differences are understandable. Crime rates and public safety
problems such as traffic control are much greater in cities than in the rural
areas served by balance-of-state prime sponsors. In 1976, the rate for
major crimes in cities of over 100,000 was above 7,500 per 100,000
population, but was half that in cities of less than 10,000 population and
2,200 per 100,000 in rural areas (U.S. Department of Justice, 1977, pp.
153–4). While similar data on the need for social services are not readily
available, social problems are concentrated and more visible in large cities.
Moreover, large urban areas are served by a variety of specialized

[5]A city or county with a population of 100,000 or more may elect to become a CETA prime
sponsor. Areas eligible to become prime sponsors are encouraged to combine with other
jurisdictions to form consortia. Counties of less than 100,000 population that have not joined
consortia become part of a balance-of-state prime sponsor.

TABLE 32   Title VI Project Employment, by Function,
City and Balance-of-State Prime Sponsor Areas, 1977
(percent of total)

Functional Area	Type of Prime Sponsor	
	City	Balance of State
ALL FUNCTIONAL AREAS	100	100
Education	10	19
Teaching related	3	9
Buildings and grounds	*a*	6
Other services	7	4
Social services	23	13
Health and hospitals	7	9
Recreation and parks	11	13
Facilities and equipment	8	11
Recreation services	3	2
Creative arts	4	*a*
Public works and conservation	21	35
Housing	7	5
Law enforcement	10	1
General administration	2	2
Other	4	2
Total project employment	(62,000)	(82,000)

SOURCE: Expanded to U.S. total based on sample of Project Data
Summaries for the 28 study areas.
NOTE: Detail may not add to total because of rounding.

a Less than 0.5 percent.

nonprofit organizations that are not as likely to be present in less densely
populated areas. City prime sponsors in the study sample used 30 percent
of their funding for projects sponsored by nonprofit organizations, but
balance-of-state areas used only 15 percent.

Occupations

The differences in the project activities between city and balance-of-state
areas are reflected in their occupational patterns. City-funded projects
employed a much higher proportion of professional and technical workers
because of the social services and arts activities. More than 60 percent of
the project employees in balance-of-state areas were in blue-collar jobs
(Table 33 and Figure 6).

TABLE 33   Title VI Project Employment, by Occupational Group, City and Balance-of-State Prime Sponsor Areas, 1977 (percent of total)

Occupational Group	Type of Prime Sponsor	
	City	Balance of State
ALL OCCUPATIONAL GROUPS	100	100
Professionals, technical and administrative	19	5
Social workers	5	1
Teachers	1	1
Writers, artists, entertainers	5	a
Administrators and managers	1	1
Other professional/technical and administrative	9	3
Paraprofessionals[b]	21	18
Social work paraprofessionals	10	4
Other paraprofessionals	11	14
Clerical workers	13	6
Typists, secretaries, and stenographers	5	1
Other clerical workers	8	5
Craftsmen	12	23
Building and equipment maintenance and repair	6	14
Weatherization craftsmen	a	2
Supervisors of laborers	2	2
Other craftsmen	4	5
Operatives	5	2
Drivers	1	1
Other operatives	3	1
Laborers	18	38
Grounds and streets cleanup and maintenance workers	12	25
Other laborers	7	13
Service workers	10	8
Protective service workers	9	1
Other service workers	1	8
Total employment	(62,000)	(82,000)

SOURCE: Expanded to U.S. total based on sample of Project Data Summaries for the 28 study areas.
NOTE: Detail may not add to total because of rounding.

[a] Less than 0.5 percent.
[b] Positions in which the workers perform some of the duties of a professional person or technician, but which do not require the formal training or experience normally required of a professional or technician.

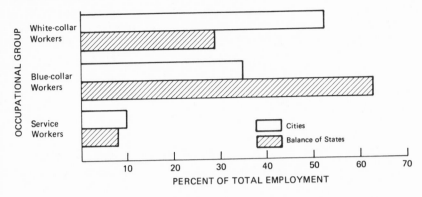

SOURCE: Project Data Summaries

FIGURE 6   Title VI Project Employment, by White-Collar, Blue-Collar, and Service Occupations, City and Balance of State Sponsors, 1977

SUMMARY

Almost all Title VI projects provide useful public services. However, in the absence of CETA very few would be continued with local funds at present revenue levels and only a third would be supported if local revenues were 25 percent greater. CETA project employees performed their duties about as well as regular public workers engaged in the same kind of work.

Public works and parks and recreation accounted for more than half of the employment in government projects. The emphasis upon these kinds of projects reflected the skills available among persons eligible to be hired and the ease of implementing such activities. As a result of these project and participant selection priorities, 39 percent of all positions in government agency projects were for laborers—about 10 times the share for laborers in state and local employment as a whole and much higher than the proportion of laborers than among the long-term unemployed. These jobs are targeted to those who have the most difficulty in obtaining regular employment, but they are unlikely to furnish the kind of training or experience that will help them obtain regular jobs or provide a career potential.

Because of their predominant emphasis on jobs customarily filled by men, public works and park development limited the opportunities for AFDC mothers and other women.

Nonprofit organizations managed about 30 percent of all project activity and concentrated on providing social services and housing improvement to low-income persons in their communities. However, these activities called for relatively high proportions of professional and skilled workers and there was a greater tendency to "cream" the pool of eligible participants.

Because of their concentration on social service and arts activities, which typically employ more women, the projects of nonprofit organizations created relatively more jobs for women than the projects of government agencies.

The patterns of project activities and occupations were different for cities and rural areas. City projects concentrated more on social services and law enforcement, because welfare and public safety problems are more evident in thickly populated areas. In rural areas there was a greater emphasis on education (especially maintenance of school buildings and grounds) and public works and conservation. These activity differences resulted in larger proportions of white-collar and protective service workers in city projects and heavier concentration on blue-collar workers in rural areas.

9 Project Process

To reach the PSE enrollment goals of the Economic Stimulus Appropriations Act in the time set by the administration, prime sponsors reviewed about 85,000 project proposals and contracted for more than 50,000. In all but two of the 28 study areas the project proposals were prepared in response to the prime sponsor's formal Request for Proposal (RFP).

Large organizations with administrative staff and experience in responding to RFPs were usually able to prepare project proposals with little assistance from the prime sponsor staff. But small organizations often required extensive help. Generally proposals that did not comply with the act or the federal regulations were returned with explanations and suggestions for bringing them into compliance.

In three-fourths of the study areas, local officials reported that the quality of the project proposals was adversely affected by the pressure for quick preparation. This may seem surprising in view of the time between the announcement of the program in January 1977 and the start of implementation in May. The explanations were diverse. In the expectation that Congress would enact the program promptly, some prime sponsors gave prospective project operators early deadlines for proposals. Others waited until the bill was passed, then scrambled to complete project proposals to meet the tight hiring schedules. In yet other areas, the proposal process was reopened late in the planning period because the definition of allowable activities was loosened after May 13, 1977, to permit expansion of ongoing activities. In some areas, the size of the allocation was unexpectedly large and required quick development of

157

additional proposals. Agencies complained that there was insufficient time to prepare proposals.

A few sponsors in the sample adjusted to the pressures for rapid hiring by working first with government agencies capable of establishing large projects. This was frustrating to nonprofit organizations that had been pressured into preparing proposals in a hurry and were then ignored or put off for months.

The pressure for speedy implementation led many sponsors to concentrate on projects that could be started quickly (outdoor maintenance and park improvements). Serving the employability needs of the participants and the service needs of the community were often secondary considerations.

THE SELECTION PROCESS

Competition for project funds occurred in 26 of 28 areas in the study.[1] The proportion of project proposals approved in the first 6 to 8 months of the PSE expansion average 64 percent, but was as low as 5 percent in some areas.

CRITERIA FOR SELECTION

After proposals were prepared and checked for compliance with the federal regulations, planning councils and prime sponsors concentrated on a few significant criteria in choosing projects. The most frequently used were the need for the service and the capability of the proposing agency. Benefits to the participants and the use of the skills of long-term unemployed workers were cited as criteria for project approval in slightly more than half the study areas, as shown in Table 34.

DECISION MAKERS

The 1976 amendments to CETA required that Title VI project applications be submitted to the prime sponsor planning council for comment and recommendation to ensure broad community consideration of activities to be undertaken. Where council recommendations were not accepted, the prime sponsor was required to prepare a written statement of the reasons. In all of the 28 study areas, the planning council as well as the CETA

[1] In Texas Balance of State and the Balance of Cook County, all projects proposed to the prime sponsor were approved. However, project review was done at the subarea level. In Cook County there was no competition at the subarea level; the extent of the competition for funds at the subarea in the Texas Balance of State is not known.

TABLE 34   Criteria for Selection of Project Proposals, Sample Prime Sponsor Areas (percent of responses)

Criteria	Percent of Prime Sponsors Using the Criteria
The need for the services proposed	96
Capability of the proposing agency and the likelihood for successful completion	71
Benefits to participants in employability development and opportunities for transition	57
Use of the skills available among eligible participants	54
Costs—reasonable relation to benefits and wages in relation to guidelines	26

administrator and his staff participated in project funding decisions, but such participation was not always meaningful (Table 35). In 16 areas, council review was not a major factor; it was either pro forma or heavily dependent on recommendations made by the CETA staff. In 7 areas, the council recommendation was the most important factor in the prime sponsor funding decision, and in 5 areas the council shared the decision role with the CETA staff and elected officials.

CETA administrators or staff were the most influential decision makers in 12 areas. In 5 other areas they shared the responsibility with the planning council or elected officials. In most instances the project

TABLE 35   Participation in Decisions on Title VI Projects to be Funded, Sample Prime Sponsor Areas (percent of responses)

Individual or Group	Frequency of Participation	
	Often	Occasionally
CETA administrator or staff	89	11
Planning council	89	11
Elected official	46	21
Other executive officer	36	21
Local legislative body	18	21
Employee union or organization	11	11
Community-based organization	7	32
Regional office staff	7	18

summaries and recommendations were prepared by the staff and adopted by the planning council with little independent probing of the merits of the proposals.

The selection of projects was an important matter to local elected officials and in 20 of the 28 areas in the study they participated quite frequently in funding decisions. In a few areas, particularly fiscally distressed cities, elected officials and senior executives decided what was to be done with funds going to city operated projects but did not become involved with decisions affecting projects sponsored by nonprofit organizations.

The share of project funds allotted to nonprofit organizations was associated with the extent to which elected officials participated in decision making. In 13 areas where officials participated frequently in project decisions, an average of 26 percent of funds went to nonprofit organizations. In 8 areas where elected officials never participated, an average of 40 percent of project funds was allocated to nonprofit organizations.

PLANNING COUNCIL ROLE

The requirement that planning councils review and recommend projects prior to prime sponsor decisions on funding added a major operational function to what had previously been a purely advisory role.

Planning council review of project proposals usually was preceded by a review by CETA staff. The staff identified projects that did not conform to federal regulations and often worked with the project sponsor to remedy defects. Usually, only those projects that were in compliance with the federal regulations went to the planning council. In 18 of the 27 areas reporting, the CETA staff recommended to the planning council the action to be taken on individual project proposals. Generally the CETA staff prepared project summaries for the council and was available to assist the council in its review.

As indicated above, the participation of the planning council was often pro forma. The most frequent reasons for this were related to time. The planning council gave its approval to decisions made by the CETA staff or by officials of the prime sponsor government because it did not want to delay or jeopardize receipt of funds. There were a few planning council officials who preferred to limit their review to projects proposed by nonprofit agencies. They felt that government agencies were the best judges of activities to be performed in the projects that they would operate.

Even where the planning council attempted a substantive review, council members said that it was not possible to absorb the amount of information presented. At best an occasional question might be raised or a suggestion made for a modification of a project design. Staff recommendations were almost always accepted. Two examples from the reports of the field research associates illustrate the range of planning council effectiveness.

Successful Planning Council Review

In one relatively small county, the CETA staff screened project proposals for conformance with regulations and for adequacy of information. It then presented the proposals and its recommendations to the evaluation committee of the planning council.

The evaluation committee reviewed the proposals to determine the nature of the services to be furnished, the adequacy of supervision, number of positions, wage rates, equipment and other costs, and the qualifications required of project workers. Representatives of agencies applying for projects attended the meeting of the evaluation committee to answer questions on the agency's management capacity, financial situation, and hiring and employment record. If the evaluation committee disapproved an application, it explained why and, if appropriate, suggested alterations that might make the proposal acceptable. This process required time, but decisions were made at this stage. The evaluation committee reviewed 200 projects and approved 143.

The recommended projects together with the committee's analysis went to the full planning council, which also considered the types and quality of services, the number of positions, and costs, but less intensively than the evaluation committee.

Only projects recommended by the planning council were officially submitted to the county board of supervisors, where final approval of the council's recommendations was usually automatic. However, one project recommended by the council was rejected because the supervisors did not approve of the services planned, and one not recommended by the council was funded because the county supervisors were aware of the proposal and particularly desired the services.

Although the council and especially its evaluation committee spent considerable time in discharging their project review responsibilities, the members were satisfied with their enlarged roles. Their intense involvement and their ability to affect final decisions heightened their interest in the entire CETA program. The CETA staff and the county board of supervisors were also pleased because the procedures contributed constructively to the decision-making process.

Unsuccessful Planning Council Review

At the other extreme, the study identified one large city in which there was no review of government projects by the planning council, and the review process for projects proposed by nonprofit organizations was a shambles. Nonprofit organizations were given only 2 weeks to prepare proposals. Further, to reduce the prime sponsor's work load and to speed hiring, the prime sponsor required that proposals include at least 50 positions. This forced small organizations to make joint proposals, which were often poorly prepared and combined disparate activities.

Each member of the planning council served on a project review committee of three members. Proposals came to these committees without prior screening or recommendation by the prime sponsor's staff. Proposals that were poorly prepared were returned for revision. The council reviewed 263 proposals but approved only 78. Because of time pressure, the council did not have an opportunity to review many applications that had been revised after initial rejection.

The planning council reviewed the proposal in terms of the usefulness of the proposed community services and job experience for the long-term unemployed. It also looked at the capability of the applicant agency. The prime sponsor shared these concerns but in addition gave "a piece of the action" to major ethnic and community-based organizations. About 40 percent of the projects of nonprofit agencies approved by the prime sponsor either were not reviewed at all by the planning council or not in the form that was finally approved. Morever, some proposals recommended by the planning council were rejected by the prime sponsor without explanation.

To relieve its fiscal straits, the city reserved two-thirds of the project positions for government agency projects to maintain or expand ongoing municipal services. The mayor and his assistants allocated the number of positions for each agency, which was then instructed to prepare project proposals. The prime sponsor, under pressure from the Department of Labor to meet hiring schedules, initiated the city-sponsored projects in advance of review by the planning council. Although the council objected to this procedure, it did not withhold its pro forma approval for fear of jeopardizing PSE funds, which were being used for essential city services. Although the council did little else in the last 9 months of 1977 but review proposals, their investment of time and effort had little impact on the project program.

Two factors help to explain the different results in the two areas. Although council members in both areas spent considerable time reviewing large numbers of projects, the workload of the city prime sponsor was significantly larger. The 263 agency proposals reviewed by the planning council for the city generally were more complex than those reviewed by the county council. In the latter case, the review workload was large but manageable, especially after initial screening by the CETA staff. In the city it was larger than council members could manage effectively without screening and other assistance from the CETA staff.

Second, the prime sponsor actions supported and used the planning council efforts in the county but undermined them in the city. The impact on final decisions of the county planning council review justified the time and effort; the city council did not receive the same satisfaction, and council members sensed frustration.

Project Approval

At the end of fiscal 1977,[2] planning councils in the sample had reviewed an average of 200 project proposals and had recommended over 70 percent to the prime sponsors for funding. Prime sponsors had approved only 64 percent of the number received. Thus, the competition for project funds anticipated by Congress did in fact occur, and prime sponsors were able to choose the better projects from a volume of requests that called for more funds than were available.

Differences in approval rates were not very large (Table 36), but nonprofit organizations were less likely to have proposals accepted than units of the prime sponsor or other government agencies. Project budgets of nonprofit organizations were also more likely to be reduced.

Nonprofit organizations received 31 percent of the total funding for projects—close to the one-third that the Department of Labor set as a guide for meeting the congressional intent. Among nonprofit agencies, the share of community-based organizations was 36 percent; the remainder went to such groups as area-wide social service agencies, YMCAsand YWCAs, and hospitals.

The large expansion of public service employment in 1977 broadened the group of government agencies and community organizations participating in CETA programs. Fourteen percent of the funds and 26 percent of the number of projects were funded to agencies that were participating in CETA activities for the first time, according to reports from 13 areas.

---

[2]Sixteen of 21 areas provided data for the period of May through September 1977. For 6 areas, the data were for a somewhat longer period, up to December 31, 1977.

TABLE 36   Title VI Projects and Costs Approved, by Type of Project Sponsor, Sample Prime Sponsor Areas, 1977 (percent of total)

Type of Project Sponsor	Percent of Proposed Projects Approved	Percent of Proposed Project Costs Approved
TOTAL	64	63
Prime sponsor agencies	67	68
Other government agencies	62	64
Nonprofit organizations	61	59

NUMBER AND SIZE OF PROJECTS

Most Title VI projects were small, employing an average of six persons. Thus the funding of over 326,000 jobs involved about 54,000 projects, and the number of proposals considered was even larger—about 85,000.

Almost one-fourth of the projects had only a single position, and the two-thirds of the projects that had five or fewer employees accounted for only 28 percent of all employment (Tables 37 and 38).

Projects operated by nonprofit organizations were smaller than those of government agencies. Thirty-six percent of all positions sponsored by

TABLE 37   Title VI Projects Approved, by Size and by Type of Project Sponsor, 1977 (percent of total)

Size of Project	Type of Project Sponsor		
	All Sponsors	Government Agencies	Nonprofit Organizations
ALL SIZE GROUPS	100	100	100
1 employee	23	23	23
2-5 employees	45	43	50
6-15 employees	26	28	23
16-50 employees	5	6	4
51 or more employees	1	1	a
Total number of projects	(54,000)	(34,000)	(19,000)

SOURCE: Expanded to U.S. total based on sample of Project Data Summaries for the 28 study areas.
NOTE: Detail may not add to total because of rounding.

a Less than 0.5 percent.

TABLE 38   Title VI Project Employment, by Size of Project and by Type of Project Sponsor, 1977 (percent of total)

Size of Project	Type of Project Sponsor		
	All Sponsors	Government Agencies	Nonprofit Organizations
ALL SIZE GROUPS	100	100	100
1 employee	4	3	5
2-5 employees	24	21	31
6-15 employees	38	38	40
16-50 employees	22	23	18
51 or more employees	12	14	7
Total employment	(326,000)	(227,000)	(99,000)

SOURCE: Expanded to U.S. total based on sample of Project Data Summaries for the 28 study areas.
NOTE: Detail may not add to total because of rounding.

nonprofit organizations were in projects of five or fewer, compared with 24 percent in government-sponsored projects of this size. This supports the observations of some prime sponsors that the requirement that a substantial portion of Title VI project positions be funded with nonprofit organizations results in increased administrative work load.

WAGE RATES

PSE wage rates perform several important program functions. They help determine the kinds of persons who apply, the types of jobs established, and the services that can be provided to the community, as well as the number of jobs that can be supported by an appropriation. Persons eligible or working in PSE who have opportunities in the regular job market will be influenced in their choices by the relation of the PSE wage to earnings from regular employment. The lower the PSE wage, the more likely that persons with marketable skills will find other jobs, thus leaving the PSE program to persons less able to compete in the regular job market. The kinds of jobs that can be created are dependent on the PSE wage because the prevailing wage for similar work in the same agency must be paid.

Prior to the reauthorization of CETA in 1978, the maximum annual wage for a Title VI project job paid from CETA funds could be no more than $10,000, and the national average could not exceed $7800. However, hiring agencies could supplement the CETA wage by any amount. The

TABLE 39   Average Annual Wage for Title VI Project Positions, by Type of Prime Sponsor and by Type of Project Sponsor, 1977 (dollars)

Type of Prime Sponsor	Median Annual Wage
ALL SPONSORS	7,690
Cities	8,830
Counties	7,840
Consortia	7,780
Balance of states	6,230
Type of Project Sponsor	
Government agencies	7,720
Nonprofit agencies	7,600

SOURCE: Expanded to U.S. total based on sample of Project Data Summaries for the 28 study areas.

average (median) wage for project jobs, paid from both CETA funds and supplements of local hiring agencies, was under $7,700 in 1977. PSE wages tended to be significantly higher in projects located in cities and lower in balance-of-state areas.[3] Wages were also moderately higher in projects sponsored by government agencies than in those operated by nonprofit organizations (Table 39 and Figure 7).

About one-third of the jobs in Title VI projects paid between $5,000 and $7,000 a year, and another third were in the $7,000 to $9,000 range. Only 9 percent of the jobs paid $10,000 or more, but 28 percent of the jobs approved by city-based sponsors were in this category (Table 40) (42 *Federal Register*, p. 2427).

Local officials in the 28 areas studied were divided in their opinions of the impact of the wage provisions on the design and operation of Title VI projects. In half of the areas, including the six in southern states, the wage limitations were not considered a hindrance. In these areas, prevailing wages for the kinds of jobs created were usually less than $10,000 and

[3]The preliminary report of the Brookings Institution on CETA public service employment for the National Commission on Manpower Policy tabulated project wage data separately for large fiscally distressed cities, other large cities, small cities, and suburban areas. The Brookings report found a pattern of higher wage levels in cities than in rural areas; project wages were highest of all in large fiscally distressed cities. Wages were also much higher in sustainment than in project positions in the large distressed cities (National Commission for Manpower Policy, 1978a, p. 113).

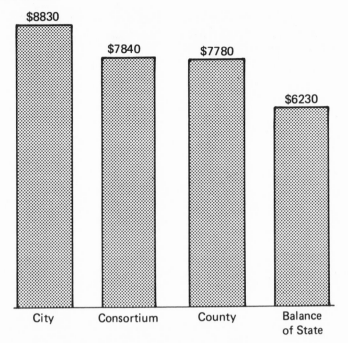

$8830

$7840 $7780

$6230

City   Consortium   County   Balance
of State

SOURCE: Project Data Summaries

FIGURE 7   Average Annual Wage for Title VI Project Positions, by Type of
Sponsor, 1977

there were plenty of applicants at these wages. Nor was the wage limit a
problem in some high-wage areas, such as New York City, where the
salaries for jobs in government agencies were supplemented by the city and
where nonprofit organizations found persons willing to take such skilled
jobs as nurse, teacher, and social worker within the $10,000 limit.

But in other high-wage areas, the wage ceiling tended to limit the types
of positions to unskilled blue-collar jobs and lower level clerical and
service worker jobs. Eight of 28 areas reported difficulty in hiring
supervisors, professionals, and skilled workers. The wage limitation
primarily affected government agencies in areas where the wage scale,
frequently established in collective bargaining agreements, put all but the
lowest skill blue-collar jobs above $10,000. The extent to which CETA
wages have been supplemented by employing agencies has been small—
only 3 percent of the project jobs were above $10,000. Eleven percent of
project jobs in the cities surveyed paid above $10,000. Nonprofit agencies

TABLE 40   Title VI Project Positions, by Annual Wage Class and by Type of Prime Sponsor, 1977 (percent of total)

Annual Wage Class	Type of Prime Sponsor				
	All Sponsors	Cities	Counties	Consortia	Balance of States
ALL WAGE CLASSES	100	100	100	100	100
Under $5,000	7	*a*	7	4	15
$5,000-$6,999	32	14	22	34	54
$7,000-$8,999	34	41	44	33	21
$9,000-$9,999	17	17	19	25	6
$10,000	6	17	7	3	1
Over $10,000	3	11	1	*a*	4

SOURCE: Expanded to U.S. total based on sample of Project Data Summaries for the 28 study areas.
NOTE: Detail may not add to total because of rounding.

a Less than 0.5 percent.

were not as limited by the prevailing wage requirement. However, they were less able to supplement the CETA-funded wages, and some had difficulty hiring at the wages offered.

In a few areas the wage levels were said to be so low as to cause high turnover, especially of veterans. There also were some reports that income from unemployment insurance benefits and from public assistance was competitive with PSE earnings (after taxes) and thus discouraged the acceptance of PSE jobs.

The differences between governmental and private-sector wages for similar jobs were seen as a potential problem in Philadelphia and Lansing, where the government scale for laboring jobs was in the $8,000 to $10,000 range, while private-sector rates were significantly less. The concern was that low-skilled persons in CETA jobs paying approximately $10,000 would be reluctant to move on to comparable jobs at lower wage levels in the private economy.

WAGE DIFFERENTIALS FOR MEN AND WOMEN

The earnings of men and women in PSE employment appear to make PSE jobs relatively less attractive to men than to women. The average project wage for men was only about half their earnings in regular (non-PSE) employment. While the project positions filled by women averaged 9 percent lower pay than those held by men and average wage rates were lower for women in every occupational group, the average annual pay rate for project positions filled by women was about 80 percent of the average earnings of all women employed full time in jobs in the economy as a whole. Annual project wage rates earned by women were closer than men's to their average full-time earnings in regular employment for every occupational group. In service jobs, women project workers earned more than women service workers (excluding private household workers) (see Table 41 and Figure 8).

WAGE CHANGES IN THE REAUTHORIZATION ACT OF 1978

PSE wages were a major issue in the congressional debate on the reauthorization of CETA during the summer of 1978. Three aspects were considered: (a) the average rate for all positions, (b) the maximum rate for any position, and (c) the extent to which local funds could be used to supplement the PSE wage.

The House of Representatives favored a sharp reduction in the permissible national average wage (from $7,800 to $7,000) and voted to limit the maximum wage to $10,000 ($12,000 in high wage areas). The Senate bill left the national average wage at $7,800. Both the House and Senate bills limited supplementation.

In the House debate the major reasons advanced for the lower average wage and for restriction of wage supplementation were that CETA jobs in the $15,000 range were politically indefensible when the average wage for all jobs in the economy was $11,000 and that CETA jobs should not be more attractive than alternative opportunities in the private economy.

Some believed that the amendments would be severely restrictive in high-wage areas. The maximum wage would make it difficult to recruit supervisors and establish the kinds of jobs that would prepare CETA participants for employment in the competitive labor market. It was also thought that the $7,000 national average would hinder the program because it would be lower than prevailing entry level wages for many jobs. The compromise finally enacted provides for a national average wage from CETA funds not to exceed $7,200 in the first year. For each area the average is to be adjusted by the ratio of local wage rates for unsubsidized employment to the national average (DOL regulations set a floor of $6,635, the lowest required average for any area).

The $10,000 ceiling was retained except that in high-wage areas it may be increased up to $12,000, depending on the relation of average wages in the area to the national average. Supplementation of the Title VI CETA

TABLE 41 Average Annual Earnings of Men and Women, by Occupational Group, U.S. Total and Title VI Projects (dollars)

Occupational Group	Men			Women		
	U.S. Total[a]	Title VI Projects	Projects as a Percent of U.S. Total	U.S. Total[a]	Title VI Projects	Projects as a Percent of U.S. Total
ALL OCCUPATIONS	15,004	7,634	51	8,598	6,968	81
Professional and technical	18,952[b]	8,341	44	11,582[b]	7,946	69
Clerical	13,204	7,675[c]	58	8,404	6,947	83
Craft and kindred	13,933	8,278	59	8,094	8,133[c]	100
Operatives	11,994	7,634[c]	64	7,024	5,866[c]	84
Laborers, except farm	10,366	7,280	70	7,759	5,658[c]	73
Service workers, except private household	10,761	7,134	66	6,108	6,344	104

SOURCE: Title VI project wages for 1977 based on unpublished data from the Continuous Longitudinal Manpower Survey, Westat, Inc. Data for U.S. total from *Money Income in 1976 of Families and Persons in the United States*, Bureau of the Census, July 1978.

[a] The census data refer to year-round full-time workers classified by their longest job in 1976 and include total money earnings.

[b] Professional and technical excludes the self-employed.

[c] Data cells for which the weighted total is less than 7,500 CETA participants. The estimated relative standard error exceeds 10 percent for cell totals of less than 7,500.

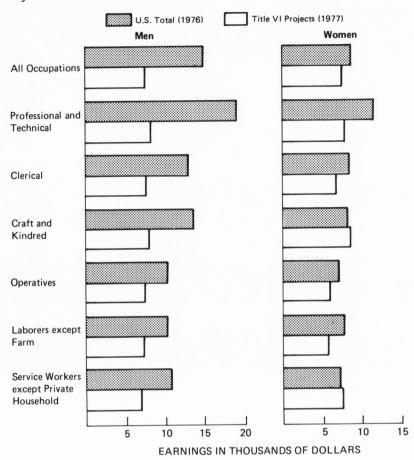

SOURCE: Bureau of the Census and Continuous Longitudinal Manpower Survey, Westat Inc.

FIGURE 8   Average Annual Earnings of Men and Women, by Occupational Group, U.S. Total and Title VI Projects

wage by the locality is limited to 10 percent (20 percent in areas where wage rates are 125 to 150 percent of the national average). Thus the maximum wage after supplementation is $11,000, rising to $13,200 in most high-wage areas and $14,400 in a few places where wage rates are 25 to 50 percent above the national average. No supplementation is allowed for Title IID, the public service employment program for the structurally unemployed under the CETA reauthorization act.

TABLE 42   Lowest Annual Earnings for Municipal Government Workers, Selected Occupations, Six Large Cities (dollars)

| City and Date of Wage Survey | Occupations | | | | Janitors | Recreation |
	Typists Class B	Refuse Collectors	Park Laborers	Laborers Class B	Porters Cleaners	Leaders
Philadelphia, November 1977	9,360	10,200	10,200	10,200	9,600	—
New York City, May 1976	7,300	14,200	15,034	12,500	8,350	10,200
Chicago, June 1977	6,500	14,600	11,700	—	10,000	—
Detroit, January 1978	9,900	13,780	13,780	—	10,440	12,800
Houston, August 1977	5,200	9,600	8,350	7,500	6,260	6,600
Los Angeles, October 1976	7,820	10,000	10,000	10,440	7,500	11,000

SOURCE: Computed from *Municipal Government Wage Surveys for the Selected Cities*, Bureau of Labor Statistics, U.S. Department of Labor.

Effects of New PSE Wage Limits

At a time when wage rates are rising, the lower mandated wage levels are expected to discourage many applicants for PSE jobs but are likely to have their greatest effect on two types of eligible persons—those receiving income transfer payments such as unemployment insurance benefits or welfare payments and persons who may have alternative job opportunities. Maximum annual unemployment insurance benefit rates are above $7,000 in 10 states and the District of Columbia, and UI is not subject to income tax as are wages paid CETA employees. Persons receiving unemployment insurance payments in states paying relatively high benefits may not find it financially advantageous to accept PSE jobs until they have exhausted their benefits. Members of families receiving AFDC or other welfare payments may also have less incentive to take a PSE job. To the degree that this occurs, the participation of two groups specifically identified as targets in EJPEA may be diminished.

On the other hand, persons with marketable skills now being hired into the better paying PSE jobs are more likely to seek unsubsidized employment as wage levels rise in the competitive economy but are held down in public service employment. This self-selecting process may have the effect sought by Congress of reserving PSE jobs for persons who are at the greatest disadvantage in the job market. It may also discourage substitution since the kind of well-qualified persons sought by prime sponsors to perform regular public service activities may be less available at the allowable CETA wage.

The wage provisions in the reauthorization act probably will have their greatest effect in northern cities where wages for both government and private industry jobs are highest and where supplementation of the CETA wage has been more frequent. With the average CETA wage reduced to $7,200, it is likely that employing agencies will have to increase the amount of wage supplementation in order to fill jobs at prevailing wage rates for some high priority projects. For example, the lowest wage for refuse collectors in New York, Chicago, and Detroit was above the $12,000 CETA maximum in 1976–1978.[4] Wages were also above $12,000 for park laborers in New York and Detroit and for recreation leaders in Detroit. Average CETA wages for Philadelphia and Detroit were below the starting rates for typists, blue-collar workers, and recreation leaders—all potential jobs for PSE employees (Tables 42 and 43). With continued inflation and wage increases, additional areas are likely to find, in 1979,

---

[4]BLS wage surveys of New York City in May 1976, Chicago in June 1977, and Detroit in January 1978.

TABLE 43   1979 Allowable Annual Average and
Maximum Wages under the CETA Reauthorization Act,
Selected Cities (dollars)

City	CETA Average	CETA Maximum	Maximum Including Supplementation
Philadelphia	7,855	10,910	12,001
New York City	8,690	12,000	13,200
Chicago	8,417	11,690	12,859
Detroit	9,662	12,000	14,400
Houston	8,338	11,580	12,738
Los Angeles	7,913	10,990	12,089

SOURCE: *Federal Register*, Vol. 43, No. 251, December 29, 1978, pp. 66135-52.

that the prevailing wages for jobs in which PSE participants are frequently used will exceed the levels set in the new PSE wage provision. Cities under severe fiscal pressure will find it difficult to use CETA employees to augment the regular work force in essential services such as street repair and cleanup, unless special job categories are created in which the "prevailing wage" does not exceed the permissible CETA wage.

Government agencies in high-wage areas will be likely to put more PSE funds than previously in lower level clerical, unskilled blue-collar, and service activities. This could have the intended effect of directing a higher proportion of PSE jobs to those most in need and may constrain the substitution of regular workers by PSE participants. But it may also mean that PSE jobs will be less likely to provide experience useful in the competitive job market.

Nonprofit organizations sponsoring Title VI jobs will not be affected to the same extent as government agencies by the new wage limits. Their wage levels for PSE jobs are somewhat lower and they are also more likely to sponsor new kinds of activities with new types of jobs that do not have established prevailing wages.

NONPROFIT ORGANIZATIONS AND PSE

Although allocation of PSE jobs to private nonprofit agencies that provide public services had been authorized since the establishment of Titles II and VI, relatively little of this was done prior to the 1976 amendments to

TABLE 44   Use of Nonprofit Organizations for Public Service Employment Positions, by Type of Public Service Employment and by Area Unemployment Class, Sample Prime Sponsor Areas (percent of positions)

	PSE Positions in Nonprofit Organizations[a]		
Type of PSE	All Areas	High Unemployment Areas	Low Unemployment Areas
Title VI projects	30	29	32
Title VI sustainment	19	11	28
Title II	15	10	21
Number of areas	(25)	(13)	(12)

[a] As of September 30, 1977, for 15 areas and later dates, up to the end of calendar 1977, for 10 areas.

CETA.[5] Only 15 percent of the positions were in nonprofit organizations in 1975 (National Research Council, 1978b, p. 179). Congress required that a substantial portion of CETA positions be assigned to nonprofit agencies. The Department of Labor interpreted "substantial portion" to mean one-third but acknowledged the need for flexibility in applying that measure. As noted previously, by 1977 30 percent of project employment was in nonprofit agencies. However, less than 20 percent of Title II and VI sustainment employment (nonproject) was in activities sponsored by nonprofit organizations.

The proportion of project funds directed to nonprofit organizations was about the same in areas of high and low unemployment. However, there were substantial differences in the use of nonprofit organizations for the Title II and VI sustainment programs. High unemployment areas implemented only 11 percent of their sustainment programs through nonprofit organizations—less than half the share provided to such organizations in areas with low unemployment rates (Table 44). Fiscal pressures in high unemployment areas led to a greater dependence on PSE for essential government services and this is reflected in the relatively small allotments of sustainment PSE to nonprofit organizations.

The one-third requirement, which applied only to Title VI project positions, forced areas of high unemployment to allocate an average of 29 percent of their project funds to nonprofit organizations. Cities experienc-

[5]See Volume 40 of the *Federal Register*, Title 29, Section 99.42, January 10, 1975, p. 2367 and Title 29, Section 96.25(5), May 23, 1975, p. 22703.

ing financial difficulties, such as New York, Philadelphia, Cleveland, and Gary, were most affected and probably would have allocated larger shares of PSE dollars to governmental agencies for public services if not for the requirement to allocate a substantial portion to private nonprofit organizations.

PROGRAM EFFECTS

Contracting for projects with nonprofit organizations broadened the range of services and increased the share directed to the needs of the low-income population. Nonprofit agencies hired relatively more women than did government agencies. Also, the likelihood of substitution of CETA funds for local tax resources was reduced by funding nonprofit projects.

However, nonprofit agencies were not as successful as government agencies in providing jobs for low-skilled applicants, and some local officials thought that a job with a nonprofit organization was less likely to lead to unsubsidized employment. Finally, participation in the program by many small nonprofit organizations increased the administrative work load of local CETA staff and slowed implementation of the program.

As noted in Chapter 8, the projects of nonprofit organizations emphasized social services and weatherization and repair of homes of low-income families. Some local officials stated that nonprofit organizations were better at serving the needs of the disadvantaged community, while government agencies in some communities were reluctant to undertake new types of services that, once provided, might create pressure for their continuance after CETA funds run out.

The activities sponsored by nonprofit organizations employed relatively more professional and technical workers, paraprofessionals, and craftsmen. Nonprofit organizations were also better at developing jobs for women, who were not attracted to, or not hired for, the outdoor cleanup and building maintenance projects of government agencies.

In two-thirds of the study areas (17 of 27), the greater involvement of nonprofit organizations in projects increased administrative problems and slowed program implementation. Many organizations with small staffs and no experience in government contracting responded to the announcement of the program. They often required considerable assistance from the CETA staff in the proposal process and, when selected as contractors, during project operation.

In response to pressure for rapid enrollment, many prime sponsors (11 out of 27 areas) concentrated on funding projects in government agencies that could enroll large numbers of participants and the requisite administrative apparatus and experience in CETA programs. Moreover, they were in a better position than nonprofit organizations to transfer PSE participants into their unsubsidized jobs.

Several officials reported that the large community-based organizations (CBOs) such as the Urban League, community action agencies, and OIC were in a better position to obtain project funding than smaller nonprofit organizations. These CBOs were tied into information networks, had previous experience with CETA, and had the staff to prepare proposals and administer projects. Moreover, it was harder to turn them down because of the support they could muster.

JOBS, SERVICES, OR FISCAL RELIEF

Although the legislation states that PSE is to provide transitional employment for the unemployed in jobs which will provide needed public services, analysts point out that the program also serves to relieve fiscal problems—either through the use of the CETA funds to pay for jobs that would have been supported locally in the absence of CETA, a prohibited practice, or by providing services that reduce the pressures to increase local taxes.

Despite the job creation purpose stated in the legislation, local respondents were not unanimous in identifying this as a most important result of PSE. Less than 80 percent of local officials who were familiar with the program chose "jobs for the unemployed" as a most important effect of projects. Providing essential services was an important result of both government and nonprofit projects, according to about 40 percent of the officials. Few officials said that fiscal relief was a major result of projects sponsored by nonprofit organizations, although 29 percent of the officials queried identified it as a most important effect of government sponsored projects (Table 45).

The belief that a most important effect of projects was to provide essential services was much more widespread in areas of high unemployment than in low-unemployment areas. About half of the officials in high-unemployment areas, but only about a fourth of those in low-unemployment areas, reported that the provision of essential services was an important product of PSE projects. In high-unemployment areas, fiscal relief was three times more likely to be perceived as a significant result of projects operated by government agencies than in areas of low unemployment.

The more widespread belief in areas of high unemployment that the benefits of PSE went beyond "jobs for the unemployed" probably arose from the greater need for social welfare services and the difficulty of maintaining normal services in such areas. A community faced with this

TABLE 45   Local Officials' Judgments of Most Important Effects of Government Agency and Nonprofit Organization Projects, Sample Prime Sponsor Areas (percent of respondents)

Most Important Results	Projects of	
	Government Agencies	Nonprofit Organizations
All Areas		
Providing jobs to the unemployed	76	79
Providing essential services	36	42
Fiscal relief for local government	29	4
Number of Respondents	(140)	(136)
Areas of High Unemployment [a]		
Providing jobs to the unemployed	76	81
Providing essential services	44	52
Fiscal relief for local government	39	5
Number of Respondents	(82)	(79)
Areas of Low Unemployment [a]		
Providing jobs to the unemployed	76	77
Providing essential services	24	30
Fiscal relief for local government	14	2
Number of Respondents	(58)	(57)

NOTE: Percents may add to more than 100 because some respondents identified more than one of the three effects as most important.

[a] Fifteen areas with unemployment rates above 7 percent were grouped into a high unemployment category and 13 with rates below 7 percent were grouped into a low unemployment category. See Appendix B.

situation is more likely to use public service employment for services considered essential and to find that it alleviates fiscal pressure on local government. In areas of low unemployment, most local officials thought that "jobs for the unemployed" was the only major effect of project PSE.

TRANSITION TO UNSUBSIDIZED EMPLOYMENT

Improving the ability of participants to obtain unsubsidized employment and helping them find jobs is a major objective of all federal employment and training programs. In the first year of the project program, little attention was given to the transition of participants to unsubsidized employment, and the short-term project jobs were less likely than regular (sustainment) public service employment to serve as a bridge to an unsubsidized job. The neglect of transition was due to a number of factors.

1. *The insistence on rapid hiring.* Stimulation of the economy through the program was a major element. Sponsors were so pressed to report increased hires each week that less immediate concerns were pushed aside. The urgencies of the moment, such as processing projects and monitoring enrollment schedules, left little time for such fundamental objectives as transition, training, or employability development.

2. *Participant characteristics.* In 70 percent of the reporting areas, local officials considered project enrollees to be less qualified than those in sustainment positions for transfer to regular, unsubsidized jobs in their agencies.[6]

3. *Duration and type of activity.* Because of the 12-month limit on projects, positions in those activities were often viewed as temporary, as contrasted with positions funded under Title II and VI sustainment, which were seen as "permanent" in a number of areas. In some of the latter areas, the sustainment positions provided experience in the regular work of the employing agency, and the CETA staff required that the employing agencies transfer a percentage of the PSE workers to the regular payroll. If the transition requirements were met, the prime sponsor would refill the vacated regular PSE positions with new CETA enrollees. However, the same commitment to transition was not required for positions funded under the project mode—partly because the project activities were short-term and also because projects were less likely to be similar to ongoing activities of the sponsoring agency. The limit on project duration also discouraged training and preparation for transition in some areas.

As noted previously, the 1978 amendments to CETA extended the allowable duration of projects to 18 months or to 36 months if the prime sponsor judges that the project is fulfilling the requirements of the program. "Limited duration" will be less of a distinctive characteristic of project PSE in the future.

4. *Limited benefits from project experience.* A substantial proportion of the local officials interviewed were concerned that many jobs did not provide experience that was in demand in the competitive job market. This was true of government agency projects for outdoor cleanup and of nonprofit organization activities that had no counterpart in the private economy. At the end of the project, the participants were likely to be back in the job market with the same limited skills.

---

[6]Chapter 6 analyzes the characteristics of project participants and compares them with those of participants in Title II and Title VI sustainment programs.

5. *Greater use of nonprofit organizations.* Officials in about one-fifth of the areas studied thought that employment in a nonprofit organization project was less likely to lead to an unsubsidized job with that agency. Much of the experience that participants gained was not applicable in the job market, and the nonprofit sponsoring agencies usually had only a small regular staff, and thus seldom had openings for project workers.

IMPROVING JOB PLACEMENT

After the hiring goal had been reached, the Department of Labor directed its regional offices to push job placement efforts of prime sponsors and local employment service offices. Prime sponsors were instructed to develop an employability plan for each PSE participant and to register participants with the local office of the state employment service at least 30 days before project termination. At the time of this study, employment service offices were being requested to make special efforts to refer PSE participants to job openings. Counseling, job search workshops, and a number of other special efforts to place PSE workers into competitive jobs were also suggested (MDC, Inc., 1978).

RESPONSIVENESS OF PROJECTS TO EMPLOYMENT AND TRAINING NEEDS

Among local officials who were queried about the responsiveness of the various CETA programs to their structural manpower problems, the clear choice was the Title I comprehensive manpower programs (Title IIB under the reauthorization act) over project employment programs. The PSE project activities were generally characterized as a short-term solution to a long-term problem. Title I programs, on the other hand, were regarded as addressing the long-term needs of the structurally unemployed through training and education. Recognizing the need to make PSE more relevant for the labor market adjustment of participants, the CETA reauthorization of 1978 requires that 10 percent of Title VI funds in fiscal 1979, and 5 percent thereafter, must be spent for training and other employability services.[7]

---

[7]The CETA reauthorization act requires an increasing share of Title IID funds for training and employability development—from 10 percent in 1979 to 22 percent in 1982.

SUMMARY

About 85,000 project proposals were received by the 450 prime sponsors and more than 50,000 were funded. The major criteria for project approval were the need for the services, the capability of the proposing agency, the benefits to the participants, and a project design that used the skills of the low-income, long-term unemployed. Decisions on projects to be funded were made by CETA administrators and staff, elected officials, and planning councils. Elected officials played an active role, especially for the portion of project activity proposed by prime sponsor agencies.

The requirement that the planning council review project proposals was a major addition to its workload at a time when other CETA initiatives were also under way. The effect of these new responsibilities and the extremely tight time limits in which they were to be executed did not, in most instances, permit adequate review of project proposals by the planning council. Moreover, it took time and attention away from the planning, monitoring, and evaluation of Title I and other CETA programs. However, the process did work well in areas where the council (or a review subcommittee of highly motivated members) was willing to devote a good deal of time to the review process, where the council review was seriously considered in funding decisions, and where the number of projects was not overwhelming.

Wages

The legislative provision that limited PSE wages to be paid from CETA funds to $10,000 for any position (with unrestricted supplementation from local sources), and to $7,800 for the nation's average, provided adequate wage flexibility in most areas during the 1977–1978 expansion of PSE. Average project wages, including supplementation by hiring agencies, were slightly below $7,700; only 3 percent of the project jobs paid above $10,000. In some high-wage areas preferred services were not provided because CETA wages for the entry level jobs were below the prevailing rates of pay. In a few areas, the PSE wages provided little economic incentive to persons receiving unemployment insurance benefits or other transfer payments.

The reduced average PSE wage and the limits on supplementation in the 1978 reauthorization of CETA were expected to accomplish more effectively the two key objectives of CETA public service employment: limiting the program to those most in need and constraining substitution. The self-enforcing wage device was believed to be more effective than the alternative of adding piles of new detailed prescriptions. There may, however, be some side effects of the new wage provisions. The lower wage, while discouraging the better qualified from seeking PSE jobs, may also discourage welfare clients and other transfer payment recipients who may find that the net value of their transfer payments may exceed the PSE wage.

The wage limitations may also severely restrict the kinds of jobs that can be created in the major northern cities where even the starting wage for some low-skill occupations exceeds the maximum allowable level for the reauthorization act. Because the lower wages may tend to limit the types of positions that can be created and to concentrate enrollment on persons with few skills, the usefulness of project services is likely to be diminished. In this connection the critical question is which of the multiple objectives of CETA PSE is primary: serving persons whose needs are greatest or providing services preferred by local officials.

Nonprofit Organization Participation

Congressional intent and DOL regulations resulted in 30 percent of the project positions funded to nonprofit organizations that were more likely than those of government agencies to provide social services, home weatherization, and community arts activities. The services were perceived as essential as often as those of projects operated by government agencies and were less likely to result in substitution. Nonprofit organizations were also more dependent on well-trained personnel—professionals, paraprofessionals, and blue-collar craft workers.

Because many of their projects were small, the participation of nonprofit organizations resulted in a high administrative work load relative to the positions funded. Local officials also questioned the ability of nonprofit organizations to transfer PSE workers to regular jobs on their own staff or to other unsubsidized employment.

Employability Development and Job Placement

The most serious deficiency of project PSE was the absence of a long-term benefit to participants. There was little training or other human capital development in the first year of the expanded program. In the view of many local officials, most PSE participants would be no more able to compete for unsubsidized jobs at the end of their project employment than before. The Department of Labor and the Congress recognized the absence of employability development and low job placement rates as serious shortcomings. After the PSE expansion goal was achieved, the Labor

Department issued instructions for the development of intensive job placement efforts by prime sponsors. In reauthorizing CETA in 1978, the Congress required that a share of Title VI funds be used for training and other employability services. A major test of the program beginning in 1979 will be its ability to move participants to unsubsidized jobs.

References

Fechter, A. (1975) *Public Employment Programs.* Evaluative Study No. 20. Washington, D.C.: American Enterprise Institute for Public Policy Research.

MDC, Inc. (1978) *The Planning and Implementation of CETA Title VI PSE Expansion Projects Under the Economic Stimulus Program of 1977.* Chapel Hill, N.C.

National Commission for Employment (Formerly Manpower) Policy (1978a) "Monitoring the Public Service Employment Program." Prepared by R. P. Nathan, R. F. Cook, J. M. Galchik, and R. W. Long, Volume 2 in *Job Creation through Public Service Employment.* Washington, D.C.

National Commission for Employment Policy (1978b) "Public Service Employment as Macroeconomic Policy." Prepared by M. N. Baily and R. M. Solow, pp. 21–87 in *Commissioned Papers,* Vol. 3, *Job Creation through Public Service Employment.* Washington, D.C.

National Commission for Employment Policy (1979) *Monitoring the Public Service Employment Program: The Second Round.* Prepared by R. P. Nathan, R. F. Cook, V. L. Rawlins, J. M. Galchik, *et al.* Special Report No. 32. Washington, D.C.

National Commission on Employment and Unemployment Statistics (1979) "Counting the Labor Force." Preliminary draft. Washington, D.C.

National Planning Association (1974) *An Evaluation of the Economic Impact Project of the Public Employment Program.* Final Report and 3 volumes of appendixes. Available from NTIS (PB-236 892/AS and PB 236 893 to 895/AS), Springfield, Va.

National Research Council (1976a) *The Comprehensive Employment and Training Act: Abstracts of Selected Studies.* Prepared by C. K. Lipsman. Committee on Evaluation of Employment and Training Programs. Available from NTIS (PS-263 499/AS), Springfield, Va.

National Research Council (1976b) *The Comprehensive Employment and Training Act: Impact on People, Places, Programs—An Interim Report.* Prepared by W. Mirengoff and L. Rindler. Committee on Evaluation of Employment and Training Programs. Washington, D.C.: National Academy of Sciences.

185

National Research Council (1976c) *Transition to Decentralized Manpower Programs: Eight Area Studies—An Interim Report.* W. Mirengoff, ed. Committee on Evaluation of Employment and Training Programs. Available from NTIS (PB-263 499/AS), Springfield, Va.

National Research Council (1978a) *CETA: Assessment and Recommendations.* Committee on Evaluation of Employment and Training Programs. Washington, D.C.: National Academy of Sciences.

National Research Council (1978b) *CETA: Manpower Programs Under Local Control.* Prepared by W. Mirengoff and L. Rindler. Committee on Evaluation of Employment and Training Programs. Washington, D.C.: National Academy of Sciences.

National Research Council (1978c) *Employment and Training Programs: The Local View.* W. Mirengoff, ed. Committee on Evaluation of Employment and Training Programs. Available from NTIS (PB-285 168/AS), Springfield, Va.

National Research Council (1978d) *Expanding Public Service Employment Under CETA: A Preliminary Assessment.* Prepared by W. Mirengoff, L. Rindler, and H. J. Greenspan. Committee on Evaluation of Employment and Training Programs. Available from NTIS (PB-284 108/86A), Springfield, Va.

Public Research (1978) *Unemployment, Government and the American People: A National Opinion Survey.* Prepared by A. H. Cantril and S. D. Cantril. Available from Public Research, Washington, D.C.

U.S. Congress (1976a) *Emergency Employment Project Amendments of 1976.* House Committee on Education and Labor, H.R. 94-804. 94th Congress, 2nd Session. Washington, D.C.: U.S. Government Printing Office.

U.S. Congress (1976b) *Emergency Jobs Programs Extension Act of 1976.* Committee of Conference, H.R. 94-1514. 94th Congress, 2nd Session. Washington, D.C.: U.S. Government Printing Office.

U.S. Congress (1976c) *Emergency Jobs Programs Extension Act of 1976.* Senate Committee on Labor and Public Welfare, S.R. 94-883. 94th Congress, 2nd Session. Washington, D.C.: U.S. Government Printing Office.

U.S. Congress (1978) *Comprehensive Employment and Training Act Amendments of 1978.* Committee of Conference, S.R. 95-1325. 95th Congress, 2nd Session. Washington, D.C.: U.S. Government Printing Office.

U.S. Department of Commerce (1978) *Public Employment in 1977.* Bureau of the Census, Series GE77-No. 1. Washington, D.C.: U.S. Government Printing Office.

U.S. Department of Justice (1977) *Uniform Crime Reports for the United States: Crime in the United States, 1976.* Federal Bureau of Investigation. Washington, D.C.: U.S. Government Printing Office.

U.S. Department of Labor (1975) *The Efficacy of Public Service Employment Programs.* Prepared by G. E. Johnson and J. D. Tomola. Available from NTIS (PB-257 267), Springfield, Va.

U.S. Department of Labor (1977) *The Comprehensive Employment and Training Act of 1973—Forms Preparation Handbook for FY '78.* Employment and Training Administration, ET Handbook No. 311.

U.S. Department of Labor (1978) *Eligibility of Public Service Employment Participants: Economic Stimulus Appropriations Act.* Office of the Assistant Secretary for Administration and Management, Directorate of Audit and Investigations. Report No. 06-8-127-L-003.

U.S. Department of Labor and U.S. Department of Health, Education, and Welfare (1978) *Employment and Training Report of the President.* Washington, D.C.: U.S. Government Printing Office.

U.S. General Accounting Office (1978) *Information on the Buildup in Public Service Jobs.* Washington, D.C.: U.S. General Accounting Office. HRD-78-57.

Westat, Inc. (1977) "Characteristics of New Enrollees in CETA Programs During Fiscal Year 1976." Report No. 6 in *Continuous Longitudinal Manpower Survey.* Available from NTIS (PB-272 950/AS), Springfield, Va.

Westat, Inc. (1978a) "Post-Program Experience and Pre-Post Comparisons for Terminees Who Entered CETA in January–June 1975." Follow-up Report No. 1 in *Continuous Longitudinal Manpower Survey.* Available from NTIS (PB-286 508/AS), Springfield, Va.

Westat, Inc. (1978b) Title VI Tracking Study: Final Report.

Westat, Inc. (1979) "Characteristics of Enrollees Who Entered CETA Programs During Fiscal Year 1977." Report No. 8 in *Continuous Longitudinal Manpower Survey.*

Wiseman, M. (1976) "Public Employment as Fiscal Policy." Pp. 67-114 in A. M. Okun and G. L. Perry, eds. *Brookings Papers on Economic Activity I, 1976.* Washington, D.C.: The Brookings Institution.

APPENDIXES

Appendix A:
Description of
the Sample of
Project Data
Summaries

The information on project activities and occupations in Chapter 8, as well as data on size of projects and part of the data on wages in Chapter 9, are taken from a sample of Project Data Summaries (PDSs) for 28 prime sponsor areas. Prime sponsors are required to prepare a PDS for each Title VI public service employment project (see specimen on the following page).

For most of the 28 areas, samples of 40 PDSs were drawn systematically—except for areas where there were fewer than 40 project data summaries. In a few other areas, 1 to 3 PDSs that had been selected for the sample did not contain enough information to be usable. In 8 areas, the 10 largest PDSs were selected and 30 more were selected systematically. A sample of 70 was taken for Texas Balance of State because of the large number of projects in that area. The 100 PDSs in the sample included about 11,000 project positions.

Employment in the sample projects for each prime sponsor area was initially inflated to the area's total project employment as of February 28, 1978, when total public service employment reached the goal of 725,000 participants.

The figures for each of the 28 areas were then expanded to national totals. This was done by inflating the data for the sample prime sponsors to totals for the United States. The 28 sample prime sponsor areas were selected to represent over 450 prime sponsors in the United States from strata classified by type of sponsor (city, county, consortium, or balance of state), by size, and by unemployment rate (in 1973). Project employment

SUMMARY OF A COMPLETED PROJECT DATA SUMMARY

U.S. DEPARTMENT OF LABOR * Employment and Training Administration	TITLE VI GRANT NUMBER
PROJECT DATA SUMMARY	39-5070-60
	PROJECT NUMBER
	VI - 77-019-M00

1. PRIME SPONSOR'S NAME AND ADDRESS	2. PROJECT AGENCY AND ADDRESS
LORAIN COUNTY COMMISSIONERS 226 MIDDLE AVENUE ELYRIA, OHIO 44035	VERMILION COMMUNITY SERVICES 1399 BIRCH VIEW DRIVE VERMILION, OHIO 44089

3. NAME OF PROJECT

Transportation for Community Services

PURPOSE OF PROJECT AND BRIEF DESCRIPTION OF WORK TO BE PERFORMED

Provide transportation services to senior citizens in their community.

A driver with chauffeur's license and physical capabilities to operate a van and assist passengers.

4. NUMBER OF PARTICIPANTS TO BE EMPLOYED IN PROJECT*	5. OPERATIONAL DATES
(1) ONE	From 12/23/77 To 9/23/78

6. PROJECT PUBLIC SERVICE AREAS (''X'' appropriate boxes))

Educational		Health & Hospitals		Transportation	X	Environmental		Creative Arts		Recreational & Parks	
Law Enforcement		Social Services		Fire Protection		Public Works		Housing		Other (specify)	

7. PRINCIPLE PUBLIC SERVICE JOB TITLE (s) AND AVERAGE ANNUAL WAGE (s) **

PS JOB TITLE	AVERAGE ANNUAL WAGE	PS JOB TITLE	AVERAGE ANNUAL WAGE
Bus Driver	$7,280.00		$
	$		$
	$		$
	$		$
	$		$

Do not include anticipated turnover
Use additional paper if necessary

ETA 5-166 (Feb. 1977)

Summary Data

in the sample areas was inflated to total project employment for the strata which the sample areas represent. Finally, strata totals were combined to obtain estimates of total project employment by type of activity, by occupation, and by other variables. Employment across all strata adds to the 326,000 project workers in the 48 contiguous states, excluding those employed in projects sponsored by Indian organizations.

Appendix B

TABLE B-1 Unemployment Rates of Prime Sponsor Areas in the Sample, Annual Average 1977

High-Unemployment Areas	Unemployment Rate	Low-Unemployment Areas	Unemployment Rate
Stanislaus County, Calif.	14.2	Kansas City-Wyandotte County Consortium, Kans.	6.4
San Joaquin Consortium, Calif.	11.0	Balance of State, N.C.	6.4
Balance of State, Ariz.	10.5	Chester County, Pa.	6.1
New York City, N.Y.	10.0	Lorain County, Ohio	6.1
Philadelphia, Pa.	9.7	Cleveland Area-Western Reserve Consortium, Ohio	6.1
Pasco County, Fla.	9.1		
Balance of State, Maine	8.9	Orange County Consortium, Calif.	5.9
Gary, Ind.	8.7	St. Paul, Minn.	4.6
Middlesex County, N.J.	8.5	Balance of State, Tex.	4.6
Calhoun County, Mich.	8.4	Raleigh Consortium, N.C.	4.5
Long Beach, Calif.	8.0	Cook County, Ill.	4.3
Pinellas County-St. Petersburg Consortium, Fla.	7.7	Capital Area Consortium, Tex.	4.2
Union County, N.J.	7.5	Topeka-Shawnee County Consortium, Kans.	4.2
Phoenix, Ariz.	7.4	Ramsey County, Minn.	3.5
Lansing Tri-County Regional Manpower Consortium, Mich.	7.4		

SOURCE: Bureau of Labor Statistics, U.S. Department of Labor.

Appendix C

TABLE C-1 Characteristics of New Enrollees, Public Service Employment, Title VI, Fiscal 1976 and 1977 (percent of total)

Characteristics	Oct. 1975-Sept. 1976	Fiscal 1977 Sustainment	Fiscal 1977 Project
	(1)	(2)	(3)
TOTAL NUMBER	150,000	127,140	145,800
Sex: Male	64	63	67
Female	36	37	33
Age: 16-21	25	21	20
22-44	63	68	67
45+	12	11	13
Race: White (excluding Spanish American)	70	65	59
Black	21	26	32
Spanish American and other	9	9	9
Education: 0-11	25	22	29
12	41	40	37
13+	34	38	33
AFDC recipient	4	8	15
Economically disadvantaged	46	57	73
Total veterans	27	27	31
Unemployed[a]	52	—	67

SOURCE: Continuous Longitudinal Manpower Survey, Westat, Inc.; column 1 from Report no. 7; column 2 from unpublished data; column 3 from Report no. 8.

[a] Unemployed the day before entry.

TABLE C-2 Characteristics of New Enrollees, Public Service Employment, Titles II and VI, Fiscal 1976 and 1977 (percent of total)

Characteristics	Fiscal 1976 (1)	Fiscal 1977 Title II (2)	Fiscal 1977 Title VI Sustainment (3)	Fiscal 1977 Title VI Project (4)	Titles II and VI Combined (5)
TOTAL NEW HIRES	242,700	100,986	127,140	145,800	373,926
Sex: Male	63	61	63	67	64
Female	37	39	37	33	36
Age: 16-21	24	22	21	20	21
22-44	62	63	68	67	66
45+	14	15	11	13	13
Race: White (excluding Spanish American)	68	68	65	59	63
Black	23	22	26	32	28
Spanish American and other	9	10	9	9	9
Education: 0-11	28	22	21	29	24
12	43	40	40	37	38
13+	29	38	39	33	36
AFDC recipient	5	4	8	15	10
Economically disadvantaged	44	46	57	73	60
Total veterans	26	26	27	31	28
Unemployed[a]	43	—	—	67	—

SOURCE: Continuous Longitudinal Manpower Survey, Westat, Inc.; column 1 from Report no. 7; columns 2 and 3 from unpublished data; column 4 from Report no. 8.

[a] Unemployed the day before entry.

TABLE C-3 Characteristics of Public Service Employment Participants, Sample Prime Sponsor Areas, Fiscal 1976 and 1977 (percent of total)

Characteristics	Title II		Title VI			Titles II and VI	
	Fiscal 1976[a]	Fiscal 1977	Fiscal 1976[a]	Fiscal 1977 Sustainment	Projects	Fiscal 1976[a]	Fiscal 1977
TOTAL PARTICIPANTS[b]	11,558	18,488	20,898	15,564	11,820	32,456	45,782
Number of sponsors	20	22	20	22	22	20	22
Sex: Male	59	59	64	61	67	62	62
Female	41	41	36	39	33	38	38
Age: 16-21	20	20	21	20	20	21	20
22-44	65	65	65	63	67	65	65
45+	15	15	14	17	13	14	15
Race: White	63	71	68	70	60	66	68
Nonwhite	37	29	32	30	40	34	32
Education: 0-11	21	16	20	19	26	20	20
12	43	43	41	45	45	42	44
13+	36	41	39	36	29	38	36
AFDC	6	10	8	9	17	7	11
Economically disadvantaged	45	51	44	56	83	44	61
UI	12	17	15	17	21	14	18
Vietnam veteran	3	7	5	7	6	4	6
Disabled veteran	0	1	1	1	1	1	1
Unemployed	81	75	85	71	93	84	78

SOURCE: Prime Sponsor Records collected for 20 of 28 sample areas in fiscal 1976 and 22 of 28 sample areas in fiscal 1977.

[a] July 1975-June 1976.
[b] Cumulative participants.